Possibilities

A Supplemental Anthology
for Career Choices

Edited by Janet Goode and Mindy Bingham

Consultant Jean Mickey

Academic Innovations
Santa Barbara, California

Published by Academic Innovations
3463 State Street, Suite 219
Santa Barbara, California, 93105, U.S.A.
(805) 967-8015 FAX (805) 967-4357

Manufactured in the United States of America.
Copies of this book may be ordered by sending $11.95 ppd to *Possibilities*, Academic Innovations, 3463 State Street, Suite 219A, Santa Barbara, CA 93105, U.S.A. (California residents add sales tax.)

Copies of *Career Choices – A Guide for Teens and Young Adults: Who Am I? What Do I Want? How Do I Get It?* – $22.95 ppd, and *The Instructor's and Counselor's Guide* – $21.95 ppd, may also be ordered from Academic Innovations.

ACKNOWLEDGMENTS

Grateful acknowledgment is made to the following publishers, authors and agents for permission to use and adapt copyrighted materials:

Advocacy Press for *Tonia the Tree* by Sandy Stryker. Copyright 1988 by Sandra Stryker. Reprinted with permission by Advocacy Press.

Alfred A. Knopf, Inc. for "The Myth of Sisyphus" from the *Myth of Sisyphus and Other Essays*, by Albert Camus, translated by J. O'Brian. © 1955 by Alfred A. Knopf, Inc. Reprinted by permission of the publisher. Also for "Work" excerpt from *The Prophet* by Kahlil Gibran. Copyright 1923 by Kahlil Gibran and renewed 1951 by Administrators C.T.A. of Kahlil Gibran Estate and Mary G. Gibran. Reprinted by permission of Alfred A. Knopf, Inc. Also for "Mother to Son" from *Selected Poems* by Langston Hughes. Copyright 1926 by Alfred A. Knopf, Inc. and renewed 1954 by Langston Hughes. Reprinted by permission of the publisher. Also for "Dreams" from *The Dream Keeper and Other Poems* by Langston Hughes. Copyright 1932 by Alfred A. Knopf, Inc. and renewed 1960 by Langston Hughes. Reprinted by permission of the publisher. Also for "Dream Deferred" from *The Panther and the Lash* by Langston Hughes. Copyright 1951 by Langston Hughes. Reprinted by permission of Alfred A. Knopf, Inc. Also for "To Be of Use" from *Circles on the Water* by Marge Piercy. © 1982 by Marge Piercy. Reprinted by permission of Alfred A. Knopf, Inc. Also for "Ex-Basketball Player" from *The Carpentered Hen and Other Tame Creatures* by John Updike. Copyright © 1957, 1982 by John Updike. Reprinted by permission of Alfred A. Knopf, Inc.

Possibility

by Emily Dickinson

I dwell in Possibility —
A fairer House than Prose —
More numerous of Windows —
Superior — for Doors —

Of Chambers as the Cedars —
Impregnable of Eye —
And for an Everlasting
Roof The Gambrels of the Sky —

Of Visitors — the fairest —
For Occupation — This —
The spreading wide my narrow Hands
To gather Paradise —

Contents

Introduction

Too many of us live our lives in boxes. Whether they are built on a foundation of race, class, gender or economic status, these invisible constructions restrict our vision. They caution us always to remember our place, limit our aspirations, forget about our dreams. Writers, on the other hand, tend to "dwell in Possibility," as the poet Emily Dickinson so beautifully put it. When we read their works our horizons expand, as does our understanding of the world and our place in it. We discover that we are unique but not alone, independent and yet connected to all living things. For thousands of years, in hundreds of cultures, men and women of every nationality have turned to literature to find comfort, joy, or inspiration.

This anthology focuses on prose and poetry that relate particularly to topics in the **Career Choices** text. Learning the information in that book will help you understand the readings in this volume, and vice versa. Questions and activities before each of the readings prepare you for what is to come. Then, once you've read the selection, you'll go on to explore and discuss its meaning with the help of additional materials. Many of the activities will ask you to consider what the story, poem, or essay means to you, and then to write about it, either as a journal entry or in an essay or story of your own.

We hope that, as you read, reflect, do your assignments, and take part in class discussions, several things will happen. First, we hope that you will get to know yourself better, and appreciate your worth and your potential. This is essential because, if *you* set limits for your own future, no amount of talent, luck, or assistance from others can take you beyond those barriers.

Second, you should begin to see the relevance of your school work — how it fits into your plan for a satisfying life.

And, once you see that connection, you may also find your classes more interesting. When that happens, your grades will probably improve. Which could make studying even more fun. This cycle could go on indefinitely.

Third, your communication skills should increase dramatically. You are after all, the most fascinating person in the world. (Well, at least in *your* world.) Reading, writing, thinking and talking about yourself and the person you hope to become may be one of the most exciting educational experiences you'll ever have. Any effort you make is sure to be amply rewarded not only with self-knowledge but with real improvement in your level of communication skills. And with improved communication skills comes deeper, more lasting friendships and relationships.

Finally, we hope you'll develop a life-long love of literature. As Robert Coles says in his book, *The Call of Stories*, "Novels and stories are renderings of life; they can not only keep us company, but admonish us, point us in new directions, or give us the courage to stay a given course. They can offer us kinsmen, kinswomen, comrades, advisers — offer us other eyes through which we might see, other ears with which we might make soundings."

Let these authors join the other people who are there to help guide you on your journey through life. There are many options available to you in a "house of possibilities." The doors that you choose to open are limited only by your commitment to hard work, your perseverance and determination and your willingness to expand your horizons, challenge your assumptions and stimulate your imagination.

You've heard the cliche, "the possibilities are endless"; well, they are. Hopefully the following works will provoke thought, delight or inspire you; they may even touch your heart.

A thought, even a possibility, can shatter and transform us.

Frederick Nietzche

Journal entry:

> Imagine that you are sitting in a quiet library on a lovely spring day. You are bored; what you are working on doesn't interest you and you would rather be anywhere else on earth. You decide to escape into the world of your imagination. Close your eyes and create your escape. Where will you go? What will you do? Who will you see? Spend a few minutes in your imaginary paradise and then record what happens in your journal.

The Secret Life of Walter Mitty
by James Thurber

"We're going through!" The Commander's voice was like thin ice breaking. He wore his full-dress uniform, with the heavily braided white cap pulled down rakishly over one cold gray eye. "We can't make it, sir. It's spoiling for a hurricane, if you ask me." "I'm not asking you, Lieutenant Berg," said the Commander. "Throw on the power lights! Rev her up to 8,500! We're going through!" The pounding of the cylinders increased: ta-pocketa-pocketa-pocketa-pocketa-pocketa. The Commander stared at the ice forming on the pilot window. He walked over and twisted a row of complicated dials. "Switch on No. 8 auxiliary!" he shouted. "Switch on No. 8 auxiliary!" repeated Lieutenant Berg. "Full strength in No. 3 turret!" shouted the Commander. "Full strength in No. 3 turret!" The crew, bending to their various tasks in the huge, hurtling eight-engined Navy hydroplane, looked at each other and grinned. "The Old Man'll get us through," they said to one another. "The Old Man ain't afraid of Hell!" . . .

"Not so fast! You're driving too fast!" said Mrs. Mitty. "What are you driving so fast for?"

"Hmm?" said Walter Mitty. He looked at his wife, in the seat beside him, with shocked astonishment. She seemed grossly unfamiliar, like a strange woman who had yelled at him in a crowd. "You were up to fifty-five," she said. "You know I don't like to go more than forty. You were up to fifty-five." Walter Mitty drove on toward Waterbury in silence, the roaring of the SN202 through the worst storm in twenty years of Navy flying fading in the remote, intimate airways of his mind. "You're tensed up again," said Mrs. Mitty. "It's one of your days. I wish you'd let Dr. Renshaw look you over."

Walter Mitty stopped the car in front of the building where his wife went to have her hair done. "Remember to get those overshoes while I'm having my hair done," she said. "I don't need overshoes," said Mitty. She put her mirror back into her bag. "We've been all through that," she said, getting out of the car. "You're not a young man any longer." He raced the engine a little. "Why don't you wear your gloves? Have you lost your gloves?" Walter Mitty reached in a pocket and brought out the gloves. He put them on, but after she had turned and gone into the building and he had driven on to a red light, he took them off again. "Pick it up, brother!" snapped a cop as the light changed, and Mitty hastily pulled on his gloves and lurched ahead. He drove around the streets aimlessly for a time, and then he drove past the hospital on his way to the parking lot.

. . ."It's the millionaire banker, Wellington McMillan," said the pretty nurse. "Yes?" said Walter Mitty, removing his gloves slowly. "Who has the case?" "Dr. Renshaw and Dr. Benbow, but there are two specialists here, Dr. Remington from New York and Mr. Pritchard-Mitford from London. He flew over." A door opened down a long, cool corridor and Dr. Renshaw came out. He looked distraught and haggard. "Hello, Mitty," he said. "We're having the devil's own time with McMillan, the millionaire banker and close personal friend of

Roosevelt. Obstreosis of the ductal tract. Tertiary. Wish you'd take a look at him." "Glad to," said Mitty.

In the operating room there were whispered introductions: "Dr. Remington, Dr. Mitty. Mr. Pritchard-Mitford, Dr. Mitty." "I've read your book on streptothricosis," said Pritchard-Mitford, shaking hands. "A brilliant performance, sir." "Thank you," said Walter Mitty. "Didn't know you were in the States, Mitty," grumbled Remington. "Coals to Newcastle, bringing Mitford and me here for a tertiary." "You are very kind," said Mitty. A huge, complicated machine, connected to the operating table, with many tubes and wires, began at this moment to go pocketa-pocketa-pocketa. "The new anesthetizer is giving way!" shouted an interne. "There is no one in the East who knows how to fix it!" "Quiet, man!" said Mitty in a low, cool voice. He sprang to the machine, which was now going pocketa-pocketa-queep-pocketa-queep. He began fingering delicately a row of glistening dials. "Give me a fountain pen!" he snapped. Someone handed him a fountain pen. He pulled a faulty piston out of the machine and inserted the pen in its place. "That will hold for ten minutes," he said. "Get on with the operation." A nurse hurried over and whispered to Renshaw, and Mitty saw the man turn pale. "Coreopsis has set in," said Renshaw nervously. "If you would take over, Mitty?" Mitty looked at him and at the craven figure of Benbow, who drank, and at the grave, uncertain faces of the two great specialists. "If you wish," he said. They slipped a white gown on him; he adjusted a mask and drew on thin gloves; nurses handed him shining. . . .

"Back it up, Mac! Look out for that Buick!" Walter Mitty jammed on the brakes. "Wrong lane, Mac," said the parking-lot attendant, looking at Mitty closely. "Gee. Yeh," muttered Mitty. He began cautiously to back out of the lane marked "Exit Only." "Leave her sit there," said the attendant. "I'll put her away." Mitty got out of the car. "Hey, better leave the key." "Oh," said Mitty, handing the man the ignition key. The attendant vaulted into the car, backed it up with insolent skill, and put it where it belonged.

They're so damn cocky, thought Walter Mitty, walking along Main Street; they think they know everything. Once he had tried to take his chains off, outside New Milford, and he had got them wound around the axles. A man had had to come out in a wrecking car and unwind them, a young, grinning garageman. Since then Mrs. Mitty always made him drive to a garage to have the chains taken off. The next time, he thought, I'll wear my right arm in a sling; they won't grin at me then. I'll have my right arm in a sling and they'll see I couldn't possibly take the chains off myself. He kicked at the slush on the sidewalk. "Overshoes," he said to himself, and he began looking for a shoe store.

When he came out into the street again, with the overshoes in a box under his arm, Walter Mitty began to wonder what the other thing was his wife had told him to get. She had told him twice, before they set out from their house for Waterbury. In a way he hated these weekly trips to town—he was always getting something wrong. Kleenex, he thought, Squibb's, razor blades? No. Toothpaste, toothbrush, bicarbonate, carborundum, initiative and referendum? He gave it up. But she would remember it. "Where's the what's-its-name?" she would ask. "Don't tell me you forgot the what's-its-name?" A newsboy went by shouting something about the Waterbury trial.

. . ."Perhaps this will refresh your memory." The District Attorney suddenly thrust a heavy automatic at the quiet figure on the witness stand. "Have you ever seen this before?" Walter Mitty took the gun and examined it expertly. "This is my Webley-Vickers 50.80," he said calmly. An excited buzz ran around the courtroom. The judge rapped for order. "You are a crack shot with any sort of firearms, I believe?" said the District Attorney, insinuatingly. "Objection!" shouted Mitty's attorney. "We have shown that the defendant could not have fired the shot. We have shown that he wore his right arm in a sling on the night of the fourteenth of July." Walter raised his hand briefly and the bickering attorneys were stilled. "With any known make of gun," he said evenly, "I could have killed Gregory Fitzhurst at three hundred feet *with my left hand.*" Pandemonium broke loose in the courtroom. A woman's scream rose above the bedlam and suddenly a lovely, dark-haired girl was in Walter Mitty's arms. The District Attorney struck at her savagely. Without rising from his chair, Mitty let the man have it on the point of the chin. "You miserable cur!"...

"Puppy biscuit," said Walter Mitty. He stopped walking and the buildings of Waterbury rose up out of the misty courtroom and surrounded him again. A woman who was passing laughed. "He said 'Puppy biscuit,'" she said to her companion. "That man said 'Puppy biscuit' to himself." Walter Mitty hurried on. He went into an A & P, not the first one he came to but a smaller one farther up the street. "I want some biscuit for small, young dogs," he said to the clerk. "Any special brand sir?" The greatest pistol shot in the world thought a moment. "It says 'Puppies Bark for It' on the box," said Walter Mitty.

His wife would be through at the hairdresser's in fifteen minutes, Mitty saw in looking at his watch, unless they had trouble drying it; sometimes they had trouble drying it. She didn't like to get to the hotel first; she would want him to be there waiting for her as usual. He found a big leather chair in the lobby, facing a window, and he put the overshoes and the puppy biscuit on the floor beside it. He picked up an old copy of *Liberty* and sank down into the chair. "Can Germany Conquer the World Through the Air?" Walter Mitty looked at the pictures of bombing planes and of ruined streets.

..."The cannonading has got the wind up in young Raleigh, sir," said the sergeant. Captain Mitty looked up at him through tousled hair. "Get him to bed," he said wearily. "With the others. I'll fly alone." "But you can't sir," said the sergeant anxiously. "It takes two men to handle the bomber and the Archies are pounding hell out of the air. Von Richtman's circus is between here and Saulier." "Somebody's got to get that ammunition dump," said Mitty. "I'm going over. Spot of brandy?" He poured a drink for the sergeant and one for himself. War thundered and whined around the dugout and battered at the door. There was a rending of wood and splinters flew through the room. "A bit of a near thing," said Captain Mitty carelessly. "The box barrage is closing in," said the sergeant. "We only live once, Sergeant," said Mitty, with his faint, fleeting smile. "Or do we?" He poured another brandy and tossed it off. "I never see a man who could hold his brandy like you, sir," said the sergeant. "Begging your pardon, sir." Captain Mitty stood up and strapped on his huge Webley-Vickers automatic. "It's forty kilometers through hell, sir," said the sergeant. Mitty finished one last brandy. "After all," he said softly, "what isn't?" The pounding of the cannon increased; there was the rat-tat-tatting of machine guns, and from somewhere came the menacing pocketa-pocketa-pocketa of the new flame-throwers. Walter Mitty walked to the door of the dugout humming "Auprès de Ma Blonde." He turned and waved to the sergeant. "Cheerio!" he said. . . .

Something struck his shoulder. "I've been looking all over this hotel for you," said Mrs. Mitty. "Why do you have to hide in this old chair? How did you expect me to find you?" "Things close in," said Walter Mitty vaguely. "What?" Mrs. Mitty said. "Did you get the what's-its-name? The puppy biscuit? What's in the box?" "Overshoes," said Mitty. "Couldn't you have put them on in the store?" "I was thinking," said Walter Mitty. "Does it ever occur to you that I am sometimes thinking?" She looked at him. "I'm going to take your temperature when I get you home," she said.

They went out through the revolving doors that made a faintly derisive whistling sound when you pushed them. It was two blocks to the parking lot. At the drugstore on the corner she said, "Wait here for me. I forgot something. I won't be a minute." She was more than a minute. Walter Mitty lighted a cigarette. It began to rain, rain with sleet in it. He stood up against the wall of the drugstore, smoking . . . He put his shoulders back and his heels together. "To hell with the hand-kerchief," said Walter Mitty scornfully. He took one last drag on his cigarette and snapped it away. Then, with that faint, fleeting smile playing about his lips, he faced the firing squad; erect and motionless, proud and disdainful, Water Mitty the Undefeated, inscrutable to the last.

---

1. What is Walter Mitty's real life like?

2. Where does Mr. Mitty's "secret life" take him? What does he become?

3. Describe Mrs. Mitty according to the information given in the story.

4. Why do you think Thurber describes Walter Mitty as "undefeated and inscrutable to the last"? Do you agree?

5. What advice do you think Walter Mitty would give a high school student regarding career planning?

6. Before we can aspire to a particular occupation, we must be able to visualize ourselves in that role. Using James Thurber's example, choose a career that is of interest to you and write dialogue that describes what one minute on the job might be like.

7. Now, complete the activity, "Envisioning Your Future" on page 14 of *Career Choices,* using your dialogue as a prompt.

8. Why do you suppose Mr. Mitty created an exciting secret life? What must he do in order to make his fantasy life real?

9. What four roles did Walter Mitty create for himself that afternoon? Choose one of these four roles and imagine that Walter is fifteen years old. Complete a chart for him like the one found on page 13 of *Career Choices.*

James Thurber 1894–1961

James Thurber, born in December 1894, was both a writer and a cartoonist who delighted his readers for many years with his special brand of humor. He attended Ohio State University, but left during World War I. Upon his return, he began his career as a newspaper reporter, working in this country and in Paris. In 1927, working in New York City, Thurber found his niche when he began his long association with Harold Ross and *The New Yorker* magazine. Thurber considered himself a writer, but his friend, E. B. White, convinced him to take his doodles more seriously; from then on the cartoons and writing joined forces. In 1933, Thurber left *The New Yorker,* but continued to contribute to the magazine. He suffered from failing eyesight, a result of a childhood accident, and by 1952 he was nearly completely blind. This ended his career in art, but his imagination and sense of humor allowed him to keep writing until his death in 1961. "The Secret Life of Walter Mitty" is from *My World and Welcome To It,* a typical Thurber creation about a little henpecked, befuddled man. He wrote a variety of pieces, among them the play, "The Male Animal," a comedy; *The Wonderful O* and *The 13 Clocks,* lovely children's stories; and *The Thurber Carnival,* a collection of writings and drawings.

Journal entry:
> On page 12 of *Career Choices,* we read that without energy (action), vision is just daydreaming. Think of something you want to accomplish in the next week. Write that vision down. What action/energy will that require? Could you accomplish your goal without action?
>
> Before reading "A Psalm of Life" complete the vocabulary lesson on antonyms and synonyms on page 23.

A Psalm of Life
by Henry Wadsworth Longfellow

Tell me not, in mournful numbers,
  Life is but an empty dream!—
For the soul is dead that slumbers,
  And things are not what they seem.

Life is real! Life is earnest!
  And the grave is not its goal;
Dust thou art, to dust returnest,
  Was not spoken of the soul.

Not enjoyment, and not sorrow,
  Is our destined end or way;
But to act, that each tomorrow
  Find us farther than today.

Continued

Art is long, and Time is fleeting,
  And our hearts, though stout and brave,
Still, like muffled drums, are beating
  Funeral marches to the grave.

In the world's broad field of battle,
  In the bivouac of Life,
Be not like dumb, driven cattle!
  Be a hero in the strife!

Trust no Future, howe'er pleasant!
  Let the dead Past bury its dead!
Act—act in the living Present!
  Heart within, and God o'erhead!

Lives of great men all remind us
  We can make our lives sublime,
And, departing, leave behind us
  Footprints on the sands of time;

Footprints, that perhaps another,
  Sailing o'er life's solemn main,
A forlorn and shipwrecked brother,
  Seeing, shall take heart again.

Let us, then, be up and doing,
  With a heart for any fate:
Still achieving, still pursuing,
  Learn to labor and to wait.

1. In line 4, Longfellow says that " . . . things are not what they seem." In your group, discuss your high school experience in terms of reality and appearance.

2. In line 13, the author discusses the concept of time. In your group, discuss Longfellow's attitude toward time. Using your birth to the present as an example of a time sequence, does your group agree or disagree with Longfellow? What are your examples of "muffled drums"?

3. If your group were to interview Longfellow, what questions would you ask him relating to advice for teenagers? Be able to site specific lines from the poem to support possible answers you believe he would give to your questions.

4. What do the "footprints" symbolize? In your group, discuss the "footprints" you think your generation will leave for the generations of the future.

5. What does Longfellow say about action? Which lines best reflect his attitude on action?

6. What different attitudes about life are revealed in the poem?

7. Longfellow lived from 1807 to 1882, a time when writers and philosophers were predominantly men. Women didn't even have equal access to education. Today our world is different. As a society, we are beginning to move towards true equality. How could the following lines be changed to better reflect today's nonsexist attitudes?:

> Lives of great men all remind us
> We can make our lives sublime,
> And, departing, leave behind us
> Footprints on the sands of time;

8. Many literary works still reflect sexist attitudes because they were written before gender became an issue in our society. As a class, debate whether these classics should be changed or left the way they were written.

The Formal Debate

Perhaps you will want to have a formal debate. If so, ask your instructor to advise you of the rules that govern this activity. Coed teams are suggested. One team should support the notion that the classics should be left unchanged and the other team should argue that they should be edited to eliminate sexist language.

Following the debate, as a class vote on the question.

> *Note: Throughout the balance of* **Possibilities,** *see if you can identify where an author has used biased language. The works have not been edited so you will have an opportunity to become skilled at making these edits yourself.*

Antonyms and Synonyms

An antonym is a word that means the opposite, or nearly the opposite of a word. An example would be:

    light/dark
    happy/angry

A. Find antonyms for these words:

    1. line 1   mournful

    2. line 2   empty

    3. line 5   real

A synonym is a word that means the same thing as another word. Some examples of synonyms are:

    dense/thick
    intelligent/bright

B. Find synonyms for these words:
1. line 3   slumbers
2. line 8   spoken
3. line 9   enjoyment

C. Find antonyms and synonyms for the following words:
1. line 11   act
2. line 12   farther
3. line 13   long
4. line 14   stout
5. line 15   muffled
6. line 17   battle
7. line 19   dumb
8. line 20   strife
9. line 26   sublime
10. line 30   solemn
11. line 31   forlorn
12. line 34   fate

Henry Wadsworth Longfellow 1807–1882

Henry Wadsworth Longfellow was born in Portland, Maine and educated at Bowdoin College. He knew several foreign languages and became a professor at Bowdoin and later at Harvard. The deaths of his first wife and child and then his second wife, had a profound affect on his poetry. The thoughtful and serious tone of many of his poems reflects his personal tragedies. Longfellow is one of America's most popular poets.

Journal entry:
> What is one of your dreams for your future? How important is it for people to hold onto their dreams?
>
> Complete the lesson on metaphors before reading "Dreams."

Dreams

by Langston Hughes

Hold fast to dreams
For if dreams die
Life is a broken-winged bird
That cannot fly.

Hold fast to dreams
For when dreams go
Life is a barren field
Frozen with snow.

1. In "Dreams," Langston Hughes compares the loss of our dreams to a bird with a broken wing and a barren field frozen with snow. What different feelings do these images create?

2. List the metaphors used in this poem in lines 3-4 and 7-8. What do these metaphors contribute to the poem?

3. What advice does Hughes offer in this poem?

Figurative Language

Figurative language is not meant to be interpreted literally. Writers, especially poets, use figurative language to help readers see things in new ways. The many types of figurative language are called figures of speech. Poets and writers use these techniques to create vivid pictures with words, and to show their ideas in new ways.

Figures of Speech: The Metaphor

A metaphor is a figure of speech which speaks of something as if it were something else. In a metaphor, that comparison is implied or suggested without using the words "like" or "as." (A simile is also a comparison, but it uses the word "like" or "as" or "than" to make the comparison.)

Examples:

> The fog was pea soup.
> He was all ears.
> It was raining cats and dogs.

A. Now, make up your own metaphors to complete these phrases:

1. The football was a spiraling

2. His face was

3. Winter is

B. Complete the statements below by making comparisons using metaphors. Remember not to use the words "like" or "as."

1. Death is

2. The clouds

3. The road

C. In your own words, explain what a metaphor is and give an example.

Langston Hughes 1902-1967

Langston Hughes was born in Joplin, Missouri. He attended Columbia University for one year and then studied at Lincoln University in Pennsylvania where he received his degree. His poetry was influenced greatly by Carl Sandberg, and by the rhythms and sounds found in jazz. He was a versatile writer and produced many short stories, novels, articles, plays, scripts, essays, an autobiography and an enormous amount of sensitive poetry. His mission was to portray the lives of Blacks in America, particularly in Harlem where he lived most of his adult life. He was an important part of the Harlem Renaissance of the 1920's. He was awarded numerous prizes and grants and is often called the "Poet Laureate of Harlem."

Journal entry:
> Is there an issue that you feel passionately about? Maybe it's something that, every time you hear about it in the news, you get a lump in your throat and wish that you could do something to help improve the situation. Write about this issue, and include steps you could take to be part of the solution. Examples of issues are: the plight of the homeless, protecting the environment, equal rights, gang violence, ending poverty, equal pay for equal work, feeding the hungry, etc.
>
> Share the particular issue that you wrote about with the class. Make a list of all of the issues on the board.

I Have a Dream . . .

by Dr. Martin Luther King

Washington D.C., August 28, 1963

Now is the time to make real the promises of democracy. Now is the time to rise from the dark and desolate valley of segregation to the sunlit path of racial justice. Now is the time to lift our nation from the quicksands of racial injustice to the solid rock of brotherhood. Now is the time to make justice a reality for all of God's children.

There will neither be rest nor tranquility in America until the Negro is granted his citizenship rights. The whirlwinds of revolt will continue to shake the foundations of our nation until the bright day of justice emerges.

And that is something that I must say to my people who stand on the threshold which leads to the palace of justice. In the process of gaining our rightful place, we must not be guilty of wrongful deeds.

Again and again, we must rise to the majestic heights of meeting physical force with soul force. The marvelous new militancy which has engulfed the Negro community must not lead us to a distrust of all white people, for many of our white brothers as evidenced by their presence here today have come to realize that their destiny is tied up with our destiny.

There are those who are asking the devotees of civil rights, "When will you be satisfied?" We can never be satisfied as long as the Negro is the victim of the unspeakable horrors of police brutality. We can never be satisfied as long as our bodies, heavy with the fatigue of travel, cannot gain lodging in the motels of the highways and the hotels of the cities.

We can never be satisfied as long as our children are stripped of their selfhood and robbed of their dignity by signs saying "for whites only." We cannot be satisfied as long as the Negro in Mississippi cannot vote and the Negro in New York believes he has nothing for which to vote.

No, we are not satisfied and we will not be satisfied until justice rolls down like water and righteousness like a mighty stream.

Now, I am not unmindful that some of you have come here out of great trials and tribulations. Some of you have come fresh from narrow jail cells.

Continue to work with the faith that honor in suffering is redemptive. Go back to Mississippi, go back to Alabama, go back to South Carolina, go back to Georgia, go back to Louisiana, go back to the slums and ghettos of our Northern cities, knowing that somehow this situation can and will be changed. Let us not wallow in the valley of despair.

Now, I say to you today, my friends, so even though we face the difficulties of today and tomorrow, I still have a dream. It is a dream deeply rooted in the American dream. I have a dream that one day this nation will rise up and live out the true meaning of its creed: "We hold these truths to be self-evident, that all men are created equal."

I have a dream that one day on the red hills of Georgia the sons of former slaves and the sons of former slaveowners will be able to sit down together at the table of brotherhood.

I have a dream that one day even the state of Mississippi, a state sweltering with the people's injustice, sweltering with the heat of oppression, will be transformed into an oasis of freedom and justice.

I have a dream that my four little children will one day live in a nation where they will not be judged by the color of their skin, but by the content of their character.

This is our hope. This is the faith that I go back to the South with—with this faith we will be able to hew out of the mountain of despair a stone of hope.

This speech is written in the style of a persuasive essay. It attempts to convince the audience to accept or consider an opinion or a course of action. Read the speech again and look for King's statement of his "dream" near the beginning. Notice how he adds more details to make the vision seem like a worthwhile goal.

If possible, also watch a videotape of Dr. King delivering the speech.

1. Martin Luther King's dream related to the dignity of all Americans. What were the roots of his dream? How does he try to convince his audience to accept his dream?

2. If Martin Luther King's dream became a reality, he said he would see it in his children. In your opinion, has his dream come true? Discuss this issue with your small group. Elect someone to report back to our larger class group.

3. Imagine that you were an adult in attendance at Dr. King's speech in Washington, D.C. in 1963. What did Dr. King want you to do? As an individual, how could you have helped him realize his dream when you returned home to your community?

4. Dr. King repeated many phrases a number of times. For example, "Now is . . ." is repeated four times. What other expressions are repeated? Why do you suppose he uses so much repetition?

5. If you were to conduct 1960's research relating to race relations in the specific states mentioned in Dr. King's speech, what do you think you would learn about those states at that time?

6. John F. Kennedy said: "All of us do not have equal talent, but all of us should have equal opportunity to develop our talents." How does this relate to Dr. King's theme?

7. Examine the very powerful images that Dr. King creates in his speech. Review your journal entry regarding injustice and create two images that you could use in a speech or essay that would help you make your point.

8. Dr. King's speech includes a number of antonyms within the sentences.

For example:

> Even though she was *small* in stature, she was *gigantic* in spirit.

> With this faith, we will be able to hew out of the mountain of *despair* a stone of *hope*.

Identify the antonyms in each of the sentences below.

> In the process of gaining our rightful place, we must not be guilty of wrongful deeds.

> Where only despondency exists today, there will be promise of a happier world tomorrow.

Now is the time to lift our nation from the quicksands of injustice to the solid rock of brotherhood.

Write a contrasting sentence for each pair of antonyms below:

light/dark
wrong/right
conflict/peace

9. Do you believe that this speech is convincing? Explain why or why not.

10. Consider what it must have been like to be an African-American in the 1960's. Then, ask an adult (who was of voting age in the 1960's) to share their memories of the Civil Rights Movement. Record their memories; what are the obvious differences from life in America in the 1990's? Has Dr. King's vision been realized?

Extra Credit Composition and Speech

Choose a controversial issue that you feel strongly about from the list generated by the class. Make a list of the different sides, or points of view of the issue that you have chosen. Take a stand, which side of the issue will you support? Read the instructions for writing about the controversial issue before starting your rough draft.

Speeches begin with the written word. Once you have completed your composition, write a two minute speech about the issue. Try the technique of repeating phrases and using contrasting words within sentences. Perhaps you would like to volunteer to deliver your speech to the class. Why not try to put the same amount of passion into your delivery that Dr. King put into his?

Controversial Issue

1. Present the issue, trying to show it rather than tell what it is. A clearly defined and well focused issue is important.
2. Take a stand; do you agree or disagree? Make sure that your position is clear, authoritative and strong.
3. Support the stand that you have taken; try to persuade the reader, using facts and logic, that your position is the right one. Present solid evidence and sound reasoning in an organized way. The strongest arguments will be made by acknowledging counter-arguments and then refuting them. Use emotion whenever possible; emotion can be very persuasive.
4. Conclusion: Take it to the universal: go beyond the issue to another, greater plane.

Martin Luther King, Jr. 1929–1968

Martin Luther King, Jr. was a minister and civil rights leader who was born in Atlanta, Georgia, the son of a minister. Inspired by Christian ideals and the philosophy of Indian leader Mohandas K. Gandhi, King struggled to bring African-Americans into the political and economic mainstream of American life. King led marches and sit-ins to protest discrimination against African-American people. "I Have a Dream" comes from a speech he gave to a massive civil rights demonstration in Washington, D.C. in 1963.

Journal entry:

Read "Why People Work" on pages 15-16 of *Career Choices*. Interview five people of various ages and ask them the following questions:

"Please respond with the first thing that comes to mind."
   "What comes to mind when I say the word 'work'?"

"What are three reasons why people work?"

How did the people you interviewed feel about work? Analyze your findings in your journal. How do you feel about work? How do your findings compare with your own feelings?

from **The Prophet**

by Kahlil Gibran

Work

Then a ploughman said, Speak to us of Work.
And he answered, saying:
You work that you may keep pace with the earth and the soul of the earth.
For to be idle is to become a stranger unto the seasons, and to step out of life's procession, that marches in majesty and proud submission towards the infinite.

When you work you are a flute through whose heart the whispering of the hours turns to music.
Which of you would be a reed, dumb and silent, when all else sings together in unison?

Continued

Always you have been told that work is a curse and labour a misfortune.

But I say to you that when you work you fulfil a part of earth's furthest dream, assigned to you when that dream was born,

And in keeping yourself with labour you are in truth loving life,

And to love life through labour is to be intimate with life's inmost secret.

But if you in your pain call birth an affliction and the support of the flesh a curse written upon your brow, then I answer that naught but the sweat of your brow shall wash away that which is written.

You have been told also that life is darkness, and in your weariness you echo what was said by the weary.

And I say that life is indeed darkness save when there is urge,

And all urge is blind save when there is knowledge,

And all knowledge is vain save when there is work,

And all work is empty save when there is love;

And when you work with love you bind yourself to yourself, and to one another, and to God.

And what is it to work with love?

It is to weave the cloth with threads drawn from your heart, even as if your beloved were to wear that cloth.

It is to build a house with affection, even as if your beloved were to dwell in that house.

It is to sow seeds with tenderness and reap the harvest with joy, even as if your beloved were to eat the fruit.

It is to charge all things you fashion with a breath of your own spirit,

And to know that all the blessed dead are standing about you and watching.

Often have I heard you say, as if speaking in sleep, "He who works in marble, and finds the shape of his own soul in the stone, is nobler than he who ploughs the soil.

And he who seizes the rainbow to lay it on a cloth in the likeness of man, is more than he who makes the sandals for our feet."

But I say, not in sleep but in the overwakefulness of noontide, that the wind speaks not more sweetly to the giant oaks than to the least of all the blades of grass;

And he alone is great who turns the voice of the wind into a song made sweeter by his own loving.

Work is love made visible.

And if you cannot work with love but only with distaste, it is better that you should leave your work and sit at the gate of the temple and take alms of those who work with joy.

For if you bake bread with indifference, you bake a bitter bread that feeds but half a man's hunger.

And if you grudge the crushing of the grapes, your grudge distils a poison in the wine.

And if you sing though as angels, and love not the singing, you muffle man's ears to the voices of the day and the voices of the night.

---

1. Re-read pages 15-16 of **Career Choices**. What kind of statement do you think Kahlil Gibran would make about why people work?

2. What do you suppose that Gibran meant when he said, "Work is love made visible"? How would you interpret that statement?

3. What does the author say about the dignity of work? Find a passage that extolls the virtues of all kinds of work, regardless of whether or not it is work that is valued by our society.

4. In the context of the poem, would you rather be a flute or a reed? Explain thoroughly.

Kahlil Gibran 1883–1931

Kahlil Gibran a poet, philosopher, and artist, was born in Lebanon. Millions of Arabic speaking people, familiar with his writing in that language, consider him to be a genius. He was a man whose fame and influence spread far beyond the Near East; his poetry has been translated into more than twenty languages. His art has been exhibited all over the world and was compared by Auguste Rodin to the work of William Blake. In the United States, where he lived for the last twenty years of his life, he began to write in English. Published in 1923, Gibran considered *The Prophet* his greatest achievement: "I think I've never been without *The Prophet* since I first conceived the book back in Mount Lebanon. It seems to have been a part of me. . . . I kept the manuscript four years before I delivered it over to my publisher because I wanted to be sure, I wanted to be very sure, that every word of it was the very best I had to offer."

Journal entry:
> Do you believe that having plenty of money would solve all your problems? Can money really make you happy? Are people who are wealthy happier than people of moderate means?

Richard Cory

by Edwin Arlington Robinson

Whenever Richard Cory went down town,
We people on the pavement looked at him:
He was a gentleman from sole to crown,
Clean favored, and imperially slim.

And he was always quietly arrayed,
And he was always human when he talked;
But still he fluttered pulses when he said,
"Good-morning," and he glittered when he walked.

And he was rich—yes, richer than a king—
And admirably schooled in every grace:
In fine, we thought that he was everything
To make us wish that we were in his place.

So on we worked, and waited for the light,
And went without the meat, and cursed the bread;
And Richard Cory, one calm summer night,
Went home and put a bullet through his head.

1. Who do you think is the narrator of this poem?

2. Why does the ending come as a surprise?

3. What evidence in the poem suggests that Richard Cory committed suicide?

4. Imagine that a diary was found in Richard Cory's apartment after his death. Try to get inside Cory's head and write the last page.

5. Can you name some examples of people you hear about in the news who seem to have plenty of money but do not appear to be happy?

6. Complete the activity called "Defining Success" on pages 18-19 in *Career Choices*. Write your own definition of success on page 21.

7. Pretend that you are a newspaper reporter writing a story for *U.S.A. Today*. Conduct a survey among teachers and students. Ask at least ten people to complete this statement:

   The best measure of success is _____.

   What percentage considered either money or material possessions as the best measure of success? What percentage said success is best measured by happiness, inner peace, satisfaction, contentment, or the like?

   Summarize your findings as if you were submitting it to your editor for a feature story. Comment (editorialize) on why you think that people responded the way that they did.

8. In *Walden*, Henry David Thoreau said:

   "The mass of men lead lives of quiet desperation."

   What did Thoreau mean? What is a life of "quiet desperation"? Was Richard Cory living a life of quiet desperation?

9. Imagine a discussion regarding what is really important in life between Longfellow, Langston Hughes and Edwin Robinson. What would they agree on? What might they have argued about?

Edwin Arlington Robinson 1869–1935

Edwin Arlington Robinson grew up in Gardiner, Maine, the "Tillburn Town" of his poetry and studied at Harvard. He was considered to be a major poet of his time in America and won the Pulitzer Prize three times. His life was difficult, plagued by ill health and financial problems. These experiences probably contributed to the theme of suffering in many of his poems about small town life. His literary technique is founded in realism, his characters are generally the malcontents and failures of the world. The most famous of his poetry collections is a volume called, *The Children of the Night*.

Journal entry:
> Read the two definitions for "passion" on page 28 of
> *Career Choices*. Write them down. What is your definition
> of passion?
>
> Love is one form of passion. What does the word "love"
> mean to you? Are there different kinds of love? What
> other words come to mind when you think of the word
> "love"?

from *Sonnets From the Portuguese*
by Elizabeth Barrett Browning

Sonnet 43

How Do I love thee? Let me count the ways.
I love thee to the depth and breadth and height
My soul can reach, when feeling out of sight
For the ends of Being and ideal Grace.
I love thee to the level of everyday's
Most quiet need, by sun and candle-light.
I love thee freely, as men strive for Right;
I love thee purely, as they turn from Praise.
I love thee with the passion put to use
In my old griefs, and with my childhood's faith.
I love thee with a love I seemed to lose
With my lost saints,—I love thee with the breath,
Smiles, tears, of all my life!—and, if God choose,
I shall but love thee better after death.

1. How does the speaker connect her love to the experiences of childhood?

2. Do you think the author represents a young person who has just fallen in love with someone at school or a young woman or man who is ready to make a commitment to their love for life? Site specific evidence from the poem to defend your view.

Figurative Language

Hyperbole

Hyperbole is a deliberate overstatement that is not meant to be taken literally.

Hyperbole is an exaggerated statement used to heighten effect and make a point.

Examples:

> The hurdler jumped so high she touched the sky.
> The stale cookie is as hard as a rock.
> I love the whole world.

A. The following are questions which can be answered by using hyperbole. Please use complete sentences:

1. How big was the crowd?

2. How bad was your report card?

3. How mad was your mom when you disobeyed her?

4. How hard are you working?

B. Find all of the examples of hyperbole used in this poem and make a list of them.

Writing Style: Copy Change

Review your lists of passions on page 29 of **Career Choices**. Write a poem that reflects your strong feelings for one of your passions. Use Browning's structure to explain how and why you feel the way you do. Begin your poem with Browning's famous first line, incorporating your passion.

Examples:

How do I love horses? Let me count the ways!

How do I love music? Let me count the ways!

How do I love sunsets? Let me count the ways!

Be sure to incorporate the use of hyperbole into your poem.

Elizabeth Browning 1806–1861

Elizabeth Browning was born in 1806 in England. She was raised in a very strict family and because she was considered an invalid did not have many opportunities to meet eligible men. *The Sonnets from the Portuguese* are a series of love poems written to her husband, Robert Browning, another well known Victorian poet. Their love story; their meeting, their courtship and their defiance of the strong opposition to their marriage by Elizabeth's father is a celebrated saga. They lived together happily in Italy, until Elizabeth's death in 1861.

Journal entry:
Do you agree or disagree with the statement that "life is but a dream"? Explain your feelings in your journal.

from *Alice in Wonderland*

by Lewis Carroll

A boat, beneath a sunny sky
Lingering onward dreamily
In an evening of July—

Children three that nestle near,
Eager eye and willing ear,
Pleased a simple tale to hear—

Long has paled that sunny sky:
Echoes fade and memories die:
Autumn frosts have slain July.

Still she haunts me, phantomwise.
Alice moving under skies
Never seen by waking eyes.

Children yet, the tale to hear,
Eager eye and willing ear,
Lovingly shall nestle near.

Continued

In a Wonderland they lie,
Dreaming as the days go by,
Dreaming as the summers die:

Ever drifting down the stream—
Lingering in the golden gleam—
Life, what is it but a dream?

---

1. Think back to the beloved songs from your childhood. Can you remember a song that included the line, "life is but a dream"?

2. If you look at the first letter in each line of the seven stanzas, what words are spelled out? This was the name of a young girl who was the inspiration for Lewis Carroll's book.

Acrostic Poetry

In an acrostic poem, attention needs to be given to the physical arrangement of the lines on the paper. The title of the poem is the subject being considered. The letters are then written down the left margin of the paper and become the first letter of each line. (The verse is usually unrhymed.)

Examples generated by students:

Just
A quiet man
Nice, liked by all.

Made to run
Always at practice for
Track, trying hard
To make the team.
Incredible
Effort!

EAGLE
Riveted to the T.V. screen
Ignoring all but M.T.V.
Couldn't care less!

Bright, piercing eyes
Unconcerned yet
Regal.
Loves cars, girls, football, but. . .
Entertains the three-year-old next door.
Yes, I know there's so much more.

3. Review your passions, values and strengths from page 27 of *Career Choices*. Then, using your name, write an acrostic poem which describes your personality.

4. Create an acrostic poem about another person. You can choose one of your classmates, or design one for a relative or special friend and present it as a gift.

Gift Idea

The next time a special holiday or event comes along and you want to give something personal, why not design a card or a poster that is an acrostic poem about that person? Sometimes we forget, or take for granted, the special qualities that make each of us unique; it's nice when a friend who knows us well reminds us of our strengths.

Lewis Carroll 1832–1898

Lewis Carroll was really named Charles Lutwid Dodgson. To form his pseudonym, he dropped his last name, reversed the order of his first two names and converted them to something more Latinate. He also transformed his complex personality. He was an ordained minister and an accomplished mathematician and classicist. He enjoyed communicating with children, especially little girls. To amuse Alice Liddell, he wrote "Alice's Adventures Underground," later published as *Alice's Adventures in Wonderland* (1865), followed by *Through the Looking-Glass* and *What Alice Found There* (1871). Lewis Carroll was also an accomplished photographer.

Journal entry:
What is your given name? Do you use this name or do you go by a nickname? What is your nickname? How did you acquire the name that you use? Do you consider your name to be an important part of your identity? Explain why or why not. Are you happy with your name, or would you like to change it? If you want to change it, what would you change it to? How do you feel when someone calls you by a name other than your preferred name?

from *I Know Why the Caged Bird Sings*
by Maya Angelou

My Name Is Margaret

Recently a white woman from Texas, who would quickly describe herself as a liberal, asked me about my hometown. When I told her that in Stamps my grandmother had owned the only Negro general merchandise store since the turn of the century, she exclaimed, "Why, you were a debutante." Ridiculous and even ludicrous. But Negro girls in small Southern towns, whether poverty-stricken or just munching along on a few of life's necessities, were given as extensive and irrelevant preparations for adulthood as rich white girls shown in magazines. Admittedly the training was not the same. While white girls learned to waltz and sit gracefully with a tea cup balanced on their knees, we were lagging behind, learning the mid-Victorian values with very little money to indulge them. (Come and see Edna Lomax spending the money she made picking cotton on five balls of ecru tatting thread. Her fingers are bound to snag the work and she'll have to repeat the stitches time and time again. But she knows that when she buys the thread.)

We were required to embroider and I had trunkfuls of colorful dishtowels, pillowcases, runners and handkerchiefs to my credit. I mastered the art of crocheting and tatting, and there was a lifetime's supply of dainty doilies that would never be used in sacheted dresser drawers. It went without saying that all girls could iron and wash, but the finer touches around the home, like setting a table with real silver, baking roasts and cooking vegetables without meat, had to be learned elsewhere. Usually at the source of those habits. During my tenth year, a white woman's kitchen became my finishing school.

Mrs. Viola Cullinan was a plump woman who lived in a three-bedroom house somewhere behind the post office. She was singularly unattractive until she smiled, and then the lines around her eyes and mouth which made her look perpetually dirty disappeared, and her face looked like the mask of an impish elf. She usually rested her smile until late afternoon when her women friends dropped in and Miss Glory, the cook, served them cold drinks on the closed-in porch.

The exactness of her house was inhuman. This glass went here and only here. That cup had its place and it was an act of impudent rebellion to place it anywhere else. At twelve o'clock the table was set. At 12:15 Mrs. Cullinan sat down to dinner (whether her husband had arrived or not). At 12:16 Miss Glory brought out the food.

It took me a week to learn the difference between a salad plate, a bread plate and a dessert plate.

Mrs. Cullinan kept up the tradition of her wealthy parents. She was from Virginia. Miss Glory, who was a descendant of slaves that had worked for the Cullinans, told me her history. She had married beneath her (according to Miss Glory). Her husband's family hadn't had their money very long and what they had "didn't 'mount to much."

As ugly as she was, I thought privately, she was lucky to

get a husband above or beneath her station. But Miss Glory wouldn't let me say a thing against her mistress. She was very patient with me, however, over the housework. She explained the dishware, silverware and servants' bells. The large round bowl in which soup was served wasn't a soup bowl, it was a tureen. There were goblets, sherbet glasses, ice-cream glasses, wine glasses, green glass coffee cups with matching saucers, and water glasses. I had a glass to drink from, and it sat with Miss Glory's on a separate shelf from the others. Soup spoons, gravy boat, butter knives, salad forks and carving platter were additions to my vocabulary and in fact almost represented a new language. I was fascinated with the novelty, with the fluttering Mrs. Cullinan and her Alice-in-Wonderland house.

Her husband remains, in my memory, undefined. I lumped him with all the other white men that I had ever seen and tried not to see.

On our way home one evening, Miss Glory told me that Mrs. Cullinan couldn't have children. She said that she was too delicate-boned. It was hard to imagine bones at all under those layers of fat. Miss Glory went on to say that the doctor had taken out all her lady organs. I reasoned that a pig's organs included the lungs, heart and liver, so if Mrs. Cullinan was walking around without those essentials, it explained why she drank alcohol out of unmarked bottles. She was keeping herself embalmed.

When I spoke to Bailey about it he agreed I was right, but he also informed me that Mr. Cullinan had two daughters by a colored lady and that I knew them very well. He added that the girls were the spitting image of their father. I was unable to remember what he looked like, although I had just left him a few hours before, but I thought of the Coleman girls. They were very light-skinned and certainly didn't look very much like their mother (no one ever mentioned Mr. Coleman).

My pity for Mrs. Cullinan preceded me the next morning like the Cheshire cat's smile. Those girls, who could have been her daughters, were beautiful. They didn't have to straighten their hair. Even when they were caught in the rain, their braids still hung down straight like tamed snakes. Their mouths were pouty little cupid's bows. Mrs. Cullinan didn't know what she missed. Or maybe she did. Poor Mrs. Cullinan.

For weeks after, I arrived early, left late and tried very hard to make up for her barrenness. If she had had her own children, she wouldn't have had to ask me to run a thousand errands from her back door to the back door of her friends. Poor old Mrs. Cullinan.

Then one evening Miss Glory told me to serve the ladies on the porch. After I set the tray down and turned toward the kitchen, one of the women asked, "What's your name, girl?" It was the speckled-faced one. Mrs. Cullinan said, "She doesn't talk much. Her name's Margaret."

"Is she dumb?"

"No, As I understand it, she can talk when she wants to but she's usually quiet as a little mouse. Aren't you, Margaret?"

I smiled at her. Poor thing. No organs and couldn't even pronounce my name correctly.

"She's a sweet little thing, though."

"Well, that may be, but the name's too long. I'd never bother myself. I'd call her Mary if I was you."

I fumed into the kitchen. That horrible woman would never have the chance to call me Mary because if I was starving, I'd never work for her. I decided I wouldn't pee on her if her heart was on fire. Giggles drifted in off the porch and into Miss Glory's pots. I wondered what they could be laughing about.

Whitefolks were so strange. Could they be talking about me? Everybody knew that they stuck together better than the Negroes did. It was possible that Mrs. Cullinan had friends in St. Louis who heard about a girl from Stamps being in court and wrote to tell her. Maybe she knew about Mr. Freeman.

My lunch was in my mouth a second time and I went outside and relieved myself on the bed of four-o'clocks. Miss

Glory thought I might be coming down with something and told me to go on home, that Momma would give me some herb tea, and she'd explain to her mistress.

I realized how foolish I was being before I reached the pond. Of course, Mrs. Cullinan didn't know. Otherwise she wouldn't have given me the two nice dresses that Momma cut down, and she certainly wouldn't have called me a "sweet little thing." My stomach felt fine, and I didn't mention anything to Momma.

That evening I decided to write a poem on being white, fat, old and without children. It was going to be a tragic ballad. I would have to watch her carefully to capture the essence of her loneliness and pain.

The very next day, she called me by the wrong name. Miss Glory and I were washing up the lunch dishes when Mrs. Cullinan came to the doorway, "Mary?"

Miss Glory asked, "Who?"

Mrs. Cullinan, sagging a little, knew and I knew. "I want Mary to go down to Mrs. Randall's and take her some soup. She's not been feeling well for a few days."

Miss Glory's face was a wonder to see. "You mean Margaret, ma'am. Her name's Margaret."

"That's too long. She's Mary from now on. Heat that soup from last night and put it in the china tureen and, Mary, I warn you to carry it carefully."

Every person I new had a hellish horror of being "called out of his name." It was a dangerous practice to call a Negro anything that could be loosely construed as insulting because of the centuries of their having been called niggers, jigs, dinges, blackbirds, crows, boots and spooks.

Miss Glory had a fleeting second of feeling sorry for me. Then as she handed me the hot tureen she said, "Don't mind, don't pay that no mind. Sticks and stones may break your bones, but words . . . You know, I been working for her for twenty years."

She held the back door open for me. "Twenty years. I

wasn't much older than you. My name used to be Hallelujah. That's what Ma named me, but my mistress give me "Glory," and it stuck. I likes it better too."

I was in the little path that ran behind the houses when Miss Glory shouted, "It's shorter too."

For a few seconds it was a tossup over whether I would laugh (imagine being named Hallelujah) or cry (imagine letting some white woman rename you for her convenience). My anger saved me from either outburst. I had to quit the job, but the problem was going to be how to do it. Momma wouldn't allow me to quit for just any reason.

"She's a peach. That woman is a real peach." Mrs. Randall's maid was talking as she took the soup from me, and I wondered what her name used to be and what she answered to now.

For a week I looked into Mrs. Cullinan's face as she called me Mary. She ignored my coming late and leaving early. Miss Glory was a little annoyed because I had begun to leave egg yolk on the dishes and wasn't putting much heart into polishing the silver. I hoped she would complain to our boss, but she didn't.

Then Bailey solved my dilemma. He had me describe the contents of the cupboard and the particular plates she liked best. Her favorite piece was a casserole shaped like a fish and the green glass coffee cups. I kept his instructions in mind, so on the next day when Miss Glory was hanging out clothes and I had again been told to serve the old biddies on the porch, I dropped the empty serving tray. When I heard Mrs. Cullinan scream, "Mary!" I picked up the casserole and two of the green glass cups in readiness. As she rounded the kitchen door I let them fall on the tiled floor.

I could never absolutely describe to Bailey what happened next, because each time I got to the part where she fell on the floor and screwed up her ugly face to cry, we burst out laughing. She actually wobbled around on the floor, and picked up shards of the cups and cried, "Oh, Momma. Oh, dear Gawd.

It's Momma's china from Virginia. Oh, Momma, I sorry."

Miss Glory came running in from the yard and the women from the porch crowded around. Miss Glory was almost as broke up as her mistress. "You mean to say she broke our Virginia dishes? What we gone do?"

Mrs. Cullinan cried louder, "That clumsy nigger. Clumsy little black nigger."

Old speckled-face leaned down and asked, "Who did it, Viola? Was it Mary? Who did it?"

Everything was happening so fast I can't remember whether her action preceded her words, but I know Mrs. Cullinan said, "Her name's Margaret, goddam it, her name's Margaret." And she threw a wedge of the broken plate at me. It could have been the hysteria which put her aim off, but the flying crockery caught Miss Glory right over her ear and she started screaming.

I left the front door wide open so all the neighbors could hear.

Mrs. Cullinan was right about one thing. My name wasn't Mary.

Characterization

1. Through narrative, dialogue and action, the author of this work gives the reader good insight into young Margaret's character. Given the information provided in the story, complete a bull's eye chart for Margaret similar to the one you completed on page 27 of *Career Choices*.

Once you've completed chapter 2 in **Career Choices**, review the updated version of your bull's eye chart on page 27 of that text. Keep your characteristics in mind as you write your Autobiographical Incident. Clearly tell the readers through thought, action, and dialogue enough about yourself so they could complete a bull's eye chart for you after reading your work.

Autobiographical Incident

Before starting your rough draft, read the "Features of an Autobiographical Incident" thoroughly.

Writing Situation:

Names are very important to all of us. You've read how being called "Mary" instead of Margaret upset and angered the young Maya Angelou. Often we define ourselves in terms of what we're called. Our names can represent our identity or sometimes our abilities or personality. Think of an incident, something happening "within a small compass of time and space," that involved your name. You might, for example, recall using a nickname, changing the spelling of your name, or adopting an "Americanized" name. Recall the specific details of this incident.

Writing Directions:

You have been asked to contribute to a booklet that your English teacher is compiling called "Names." Write an Autobiographical Incident about a time when your first name seemed especially important to you. Your readers will want to know specifically who was involved in this incident, what happened, where and when it took place, and the significance this incident had for you. Write your incident in an interesting and colorful way so that your readers will enjoy it and understand just how you felt.

Features Of An Autobiographical Incident

"My Name is Margaret" is a good example of an Autobiographical Incident. The Autobiographical Incident is a
story about a specific occurrence in the writer's life. The story
takes place in a short period of time, within minutes or hours,
or a day or two. The sequence of the action is clear. The
significance of the incident itself for the writer is clear. The
incident is revealed in rich sensory detail which allows the
reader to experience the events and share the feelings of
the writer.

The main features of this style of writing are:

1. Writers usually choose the first person point of view to tell
    about a personal experience; they tell the story as "I" or
    "we."

2. Tell the story as a straightforward chronological narrative,
    let the incident unfold as it happened. One technique is
    to frame an event by beginning and ending in the present
    and using a flashback for the event itself.

3. The beginning of the story captures the reader's interest and
    makes him want to read on. (Notice Maya Angelou's
    opening paragraphs.)

4. To sustain the reader's interest, create tension.

5. The narrative should be coherent and complete, and give
    enough information to show what happened. The reader
    should be able to move smoothly through the story
    without confusion.

6. Use sensory detail to present important scenes, people and
    feelings. Specifically name and describe the features and
    objects at the scene of the incident.

7. The ending should be integrated into the story, not tacked on.

Maya Angelou 1928–

Maya Angelou was born in 1928 in the South, but followed her mother west during the 1940's. After studying dance, she was active in the theater, toured Africa and Europe for the State Department, produced a television series on African traditions and published two volumes of poetry. *I Know Why the Caged Bird Sings*, was written in 1970 and was the first volume of her autobiography. It recalls her southern childhood and coming of age in the west, and shows what one African-American woman found in the Golden State.

Journal entry:
Have you ever felt caged in or trapped in a situation?
How did you feel? What did you do about it?

Complete the lesson on personification through Part II
and then read "Sympathy" and complete Part III.

Sympathy

by Paul Laurence Dunbar

I know what the caged bird feels, alas!
    When the sun is bright on the upland slopes;
When the wind stirs soft through the springing grass,
And the river flows like a stream of glass;
    When the first bird sings and the first bud opes,
And the faint perfume from its chalice steals—
I know what the caged bird feels!

I know why the caged bird beats his wing
    Till its blood is red on the cruel bars;
For he must fly back to his perch and cling
When he fain would be on the bough a-swing;
    And a pain still throbs in the old, old scars
And they pulse again with a keener sting—
I know why he beats his wing!

Continued

I know why the caged bird sings, ah me,
    When his wing is bruised and his bosom sore,—
When he beats his bars and he would be free;
It is not a carol of joy or glee,
    But a prayer that he sends from his heart's deep core,
But a plea, that upward to Heaven he flings—
I know why the caged bird sings!

---

1. What changes in the poem from stanza one to stanza two?

2. Why do you think that the poet presents the lovely images from nature and then contrasts them with the brutal images of the trapped bird?

3. Paul Dunbar was an African-American who lived from 1872 to 1906; given that information, what could this poem be alluding to?

4. One way that many adults feel "caged in" is by their choice (or lack of choice) of a career. Have you ever heard anyone express this feeling of frustration about their job? Can you describe how this would make someone feel?

5. From a teenager's perspective, can you describe an experience where you knew why "the caged bird sings."

Personification

Personification is a type of figurative language in which objects, or nonhuman subjects, are given human qualities. Personification is effective in making things or ideas seem alive, as if they were human.

Notice how Joyce Kilmer personifies a tree in the following excerpt from "Trees":

> A tree whose hungry mouth is prest
> Against the earth's sweet flowing breast;
>
> A tree who looks at God all day,
> And lifts her leafy arms to pray;

a. Do trees have mouths or arms? Who has those features? Can trees look or pray? Who can do those things?

b. Why did Kilmer give the trees human qualities?

Remember, when you write about objects, things, ideas, and animals as if they were human, you are using personification.

Examples:

> The sun *smiled* down upon us.
>
> The chair sat *smugly* in the corner.

I. Read the following statements and replace the italicized words or phrases with human actions.

1. The wind *blew* in the night.
2. The lawnmower *made a noise.*
3. The trees *fluttered* in the breeze.

II. Now, read the following statements and questions. When you answer the questions, use personification in your answers to make things come alive with human qualities.

Example:

> Instead of—The house was at the side of the hill.
>
> It becomes—The house clung for dear life to the side of the hill.

4. The happy family moved out of their house. *How did the house feel?*

5. The boy outgrew his toys. *How did the toys feel?*

6. The car was dirty and neglected. *How did the car feel?*

III. Finally, underline all of the examples of personification found in "Sympathy."

IV. In your own words, define personification.

Paul Laurence Dunbar 1872–1906

Paul Laurence Dunbar was born in Dayton, Ohio. He was the son of former slaves who had been freed before the outbreak of the Civil War. He was the first African-American writer to support himself through his writing. He wrote poems, short stories and novels. In "Sympathy," the frustration of not being free is even more relevant when the reader realizes that the son of former slaves wrote it.

Journal entry:
   Complete the exercise on page 52 of *Career Choices*.
   Were any of the messages limiting or negative? Can you
   think of a situation where you allowed someone else's
   opinions or ideas to overly influence what you tried to
   do? Write about the situation and your resulting feelings.

Life

by Nan Terrell Reed

THEY TOLD ME that Life could be just what I made it—
   Life could be fashioned and worn like a gown;
I, the designer; mine the decision
   Whether to wear it with bonnet or crown.

And so I selected the prettiest pattern—
   Life should be made of the rosiest hue—
Something unique, and a bit out of fashion,
   One that perhaps would be chosen by few.

But other folks came and they leaned o'er my shoulder;
   Somebody questioned the ultimate cost;
Somebody tangled the thread I was using;
   One day I found that my scissors were lost.

And somebody claimed the material faded;
   Somebody said I'd be tired ere 'twas worn;
Somebody's fingers, too pointed and spiteful,
   Snatched at the cloth, and I saw it was torn.

Continued

Oh! somebody tried to do all the sewing,
　　Wanting always to advise or condone.
Here is my life, the product of many;
　　Where is that gown I could fashion—alone?

---

1. What is the theme of Nan Terrell Reed's poem?

2. Read again the passage from page 53 of **Career Choices**?:

   "How much importance should you place on other people's opinions of you and their plans for your life? Should you have to live up to other people's goals and ideals? Whose life is it anyway?"

   How does the poem "Life" give an example of what can happen when others have too great an influence on our lives?

3. What similes and metaphors does Reed use to make comparisons?

4. Review your responses on page 52 of **Career Choices**. If anyone in your life has given you limiting messages, choose one or two lines from the poem, "Life," that best describes them or their involvement.

5. What personal characteristics are required of us to choose our own paths for ourselves, while not over valuing others' opinions?

6. Reed chose the art of sewing to make her point about planning for life. What issues do you think Reed would want society to address regarding the career planning process for females? What differences have you noted regarding career planning for males and females? Should there be differences in the process?

Figurative Language

The Simile

The simile is a figure of speech that makes a direct comparison between two subjects using either like or as. Similes are used frequently by poets.

> *Examples:*
>
> > The fog was as thick as soup.
> >
> > She treated him like a dog.
> >
> > He was as big as a house.

A. Now, complete these sentences:

1. He is as stubborn as

2. The tree was like

3. She was as busy as

4. School was like

B. Let's see how creative your similes can be. Complete these statements by making comparisons:

1. The truck

2. The students

Journal entry:
Imagine the following situation: You have worked day and night for several years and have discovered a cure for arthritis. Although you were trained in traditional medicine, your method might be considered "new age" or "holistic" in its approach. You have conducted extensive studies and are convinced that you have made an important discovery. Over 80% of your patients are cured or have experienced significant improvement. You presented your findings at a national medical convention and the audience of medical professionals sat in stunned silence at the end. You are shocked to realize that they think you are practicing quackery. Three of your colleagues paid you a visit to advise you to drop this foolishness and discontinue your project before it ruins your reputation. What will you do?

You may find it helpful to complete the vocabulary lesson before you read Emerson's essay.

from *Self-Reliance*
by Ralph Waldo Emerson

There is a time in every man's education when he arrives at the conviction that envy is ignorance; that imitation is suicide; that he must take himself for better, for worse, as his portion; that though the wide universe is full of good, no kernel of nourishing corn can come to him but through his toil bestowed on that plot of ground which is given to him to till. The power which resides in him is new in nature, and none but he knows what that is which he can do, nor does he know until he has tried. Not for nothing one face, one character, one fact makes much impression on him, and another none. This sculpture in the memory is not without preestablished harmony. The eye was placed where one ray should fall, that it might testify of that particular ray. We but half express ourselves, and are ashamed of that divine idea which each of us represents. It may be safely trusted as proportionate and of good issues, so it be faithfully imparted, but God will not have his work made manifest by cowards. A man is relieved and gay when he has put his heart into his work and done his best; but what he has said or done otherwise, shall give him no peace. It is a deliverance which does not deliver. In the attempt his genius deserts him; no muse befriends; no invention, no hope.

Trust thyself: every heart vibrates to that iron string. Accept the place the divine providence has found for you; the society of your contemporaries, the connection of events. Great men have always done so and confided themselves childlike to the genius of their age, betraying their perception that the absolutely trustworthy was stirring at their heart, working through their hands, predominating in all their being. And we are now men, and must accept in the highest mind the same transcendent destiny: and not minors and invalids in a protected corner, but guides, redeemers, and benefactors, obeying the Almighty effort and advancing on Chaos and the Dark. . . .

Society everywhere is in conspiracy against the manhood of every one of its members. Society is a joint-stock company in which the members agree for the better securing of his bread to each shareholder, to surrender the liberty and culture of the eater. The virtue in most request is conformity. Self-reliance is its aversion. It loves not realities and creators, but names and customs.

Whoso would be a man must be a non-conformist. He who would gather immortal palms must not be hindered by the name of goodness, but must explore if it be goodness.

Nothing is at last sacred but the integrity of our own mind. Absolve you to yourself, and you shall have the suffrage of the world. . . .

A foolish consistency is the hobgoblin of little minds, adored by little statesmen and philosophers and divines. With consistency a great soul has simply nothing to do. He may as well concern himself with his shadow on the wall. Speak what you think now in hard words and tomorrow speak what tomorrow thinks in hard words again, though it contradict everything you said today. "Ah, so you shall be sure to be misunderstood?" — Is it so bad, then, to be misunderstood? Pythagoras was misunderstood, and Socrates, and Jesus, and Luther, and Copernicus, and Galileo, and Newton, and every pure and wise spirit that ever took flesh. To be great is to be misunderstood. . . .

---

1. Find one passage from the essay that impresses you the most; explain what the passage means to you.

2. What does Emerson mean when he writes: "A man is relieved and gay when he has put his heart into his work and done his best; but what he has said or done otherwise, shall give him no peace."? Explain fully.

3. What does Emerson mean when he says that "to be great is to be misunderstood"?

4. Examine the first paragraph; at what conviction does every person arrive?

5. Examine the second paragraph; what must every person accept?

6. How is society described?

7. What is sacred?

8. What does Emerson mean when he says, "A foolish consistency is the hobgoblin of little minds"?

9. Can you think of any "foolish consistencies" in your life? Review page 52 of **Career Choices**. Could any of the messages be "foolish consistencies"? Which ones and by whom?

10. What comment does Emerson make about nonconformity? Can you think of any nonconformists in today's world? What kinds of careers would probably be most satisfying for a nonconformist? Was there ever a time when you were a nonconformist?

11. Whom must we trust?

Composition

In light of the excerpt from the essay "Self-Reliance" by Emerson, respond to the following quotation in a fully developed essay:

> *If a man does not keep pace with his companions, perhaps it is because he hears a different drummer. Let him step to the music which he hears, however measured or far away.*
>
> Henry David Thoreau

If you like, first change the language of the quote to make it gender inclusive.

Vocabulary

Find a synonym or an antonym (identify which you have chosen) for each of the following words:

1. consistency

2. nonconformist

3. nourishing

4. sculpture

5. harmony
6. divine
7. contemporaries
8. perception
9. benefactors
10. conspiracy
11. immortal
12. philosophers

Ralph Waldo Emerson 1803–1882

Ralph Waldo Emerson was born in Boston, Massachusetts, and later lived in Concord. A graduate of Harvard's Divinity School, he was appointed a Unitarian minister. He preached and lectured widely and was recognized by the great thinkers of his day. His ideas are considered to be the core of the Transcendental Movement and essays such as "Self-Reliance" mark him as a major writer. His many lectures, essays and poems appear in *The Complete Works*.

Journal entry:
List some of the people you know who are:

in their sixties
in their seventies
in their eighties

Think about these people for a few minutes. Do you notice changes (emotionally, psychologically, physically) with each different decade? What seems to be most important to someone in their sixties, in their seventies, in their eighties?

Growing Older

by R. G. Wells

A LITTLE MORE TIRED at the close of day,
A little more anxious to have our way,
A little less ready to scold and blame,
A little more care for a brother's name;
And so we are nearing the journey's end,
Where time and eternity meet and blend.

A little less care for bonds or gold,
A little more zeal for the days of old;
A broader view and a saner mind,
And a little more love for all mankind;
And so we are faring down the way
That leads to the gates of a better day.

Continued

A little more love for the friends of youth,
A little more zeal for established truth,
A little more charity in our views,
A little less thirst for the daily news;
And so we are folding our tents away
And passing in silence at close of day.

A little more leisure to sit and dream,
A little more real the things unseen,
A little nearer to those ahead,
With visions of those long loved and dead;
And so we are going where all must go—
To the place the living may never know.

A little more laughter, a few more tears,
And we shall have told our increasing years.
The book is closed and the prayers are said,
And we are part of the countless dead;
Thrice happy, then, if some soul can say,
"I live because of their help on the way."

---

1. Have you ever thought about what your life will be like when you are older? Imagine you are seventy. Will you be retired? Will you have grandchildren? Will you be content? Will you be able to reflect upon your life and feel satisfied?

2. Re-read the last six lines of the poem. What desire/belief does the narrator express?

3. Your instructor may take you through a guided visualization activity that could help you identify what will make you feel successful and contented with your life. Before starting this activity, re-read "Growing Older" to help you visualize your senior citizen years.

4. Teens and senior citizens are often considered "misunderstood" and even "hard to handle." It is interesting to note that teens and seniors also share the fastest growing suicide rates in this nation. Write a short paper comparing the problems teenagers and senior citizens have in common.

Journal entry:
Complete the activity on page 61 of *Career Choices*. At this time in your life, what is your mission?

I Shall Not Pass This Way Again

Anonymous

Through this toilsome world, alas!
Once and only once I pass;
If a kindness I may show,
If a good deed I may do
To a suffering fellow man,
Let me do it while I can.
No delay, for it is plain
I shall not pass this way again.

---

1. When do you think that this poem was written?
2. What words do you find in the poem that are rarely used today?
3. What is the message of this poem?
4. What rhyme scheme is used?
5. This is a simple poem which contains many words that are rarely heard today. Using more modern English, re-write this poem to make it sound like it was written in the 1990's. Try to follow the rhyme scheme if you can.

6. Using the theme that you have identified as your mission in life, complete a copy change of this poem. Leave the first two and the last two lines the same, but change the middle verses to reflect your mission and identity.

Through this toilsome world, alas!
Once and only once I pass;

_____

_____

_____

_____

No delay, for it is plain
I shall not pass this way again.

Why not share your poems with your classmates?
Write your poem on a large piece of paper or typeset it at the computer lab. Using colored pencils, crayons, pastels or paints, decorate it with an artistic border. Hang the poems around the classroom for everyone to enjoy.

Journal entry:
> What are the simple things, (flowers blooming outside your door, a lovely view, hills, the ocean or even re-runs, a bag of chips, a snowball fight or just "hanging out") that you enjoy in your daily life? Jot down the names of a few of your favorite things.

Red Geraniums

by Martha Haskell Clark

Life did not bring me silken gowns,
Nor jewels for my hair,
Nor signs of gabled foreign towns
In distant countries fair,
But I can glimpse, beyond my pane, a green and friendly hill,
And red geraniums aflame upon my window sill.

The brambled cares of everyday,
The tiny humdrum things,
May bind my feet when they would stray,
But still my heart has wings
While red geraniums are bloomed against my window glass,
And low above my green-sweet hill the gypsy wind-clouds pass.

And if my dreamings ne'er come true,
The brightest and the best,
But leave me lone my journey through,
I'll set my heart at rest,
And thank God for home-sweet things, a green and friendly hill,
And red geraniums aflame upon my window sill.

1. Reflect for a moment immediately after reading this poem; what are you feeling right now? Describe those feelings. Then, examine the list of the common things that you enjoy in your daily life and describe how they make you feel when you see or experience them.

2. Do you think that most people appreciate their surroundings? Why do you think that people often take for granted the beauty that is all around them?

3. How do you experience nature? What kind of effect does it have on you? Do you ever seek out natural wonders (a flower, sunset, forest, quiet brook) when you are feeling overwhelmed or out of balance?

4. Review the information on the Modified Maslow Triangle, pages 66 to 71 in *Career Choices*. Complete a diagram of Martha Haskell Clark's life; do you think that it is in balance? Explain why or why not.

Writer's Notebook

Keep a journal to record special events and ideas. This could be a shooting star that you see and want to remember, something that you've heard, a quote that you thought was special and want to record. There's a delightful book called *I'm in Charge of Celebrations* by Byrd Baylor (published by Scribner's), which explains the process well. The writer's notebook is something that you should keep with you, just like you would a camera, to have handy when those special moments happen and you can record them. Later, you can refer to your writer's notebook when you need a topic to write about or inspiration to keep going.

Journal entry:
  Read Ivy Elm's story on pages 74 and 75 in *Career Choices*. Can you think of any other characters in real life, or in fiction, who have lives similar to Ivy Elm's? Does Ivy live a balanced lifestyle? How happy do you think she is?

The Mills of the Gods

Anonymous

He was the slave of Ambition
And he vowed to the Gods above
To sell his soul to perdition
For Fortune, Fame, and Love.
"Three Wishes," he cried,
And the Devil replied:
"Fortune is a fickle one,
Often wooed but seldom won,
Ever changing like the sun;
Still, I think it can be done.
You have a friend, a rich one too;
Kill him! His wealth is willed to you."
Ambition fled. He paused awhile,
But, daunted by the Devil's smile,
He killed his friend to gain his aim,
Then bowed his head in grief and shame;
But the Devil cried, "It's all in the game.
You wanted Fortune, Love, and Fame,
And so, I came.
Three wishes through your life shall run,
Behold, I've given you Number One."

And the Gods on high, with a watchful eye,
Looked down on the ways of man,
With their hopes and fears through the weary years
Since the days of the world began.
And the man, he prayed, for the soul betrayed
Had breathed a parting call:
"Though the Mills of the Gods grind slowly,
Yet they grind exceeding small."

Urged by the spur of Ambition,
With the Devil still as his guide,
He now sought social position,
For wealth had brought him pride.
"Bring Fame," cried the man,
So the Devil began:
"Fame is but an accident,
Often sought but seldom sent,
Still, I think we're on the scent.

You know a genius gone insane;
Go steal the product of his brain."
The man obeyed, then cried, "Begone!
From crime to crime you lead me on,
To kill a friend whose smile was glad,
To rob a genius driven mad
Through want. Oh God! Am I that bad?"
But the Devil cried, "What luck you've had!
You're famous, lad!
Three wishes run your whole life through,
Behold, I've given you Number Two."
And the Gods looked down with an angry frown
Till Satan fled their scorn.
For the Devil may play with the common clay,
But genius is heaven-born.

Continued

And the man grew bold with his Fame and Gold,
And cried, "Well, after all,
The Mills of the Gods grind slowly,
If they ever grind at all."

Men, good or bad, are but human,
And he, like the rest, wanted love.
So the Devil soon brought him the woman
As fair as an angel above.
"I love you," he cried,
But the woman replied,
"Love is such an empty word,
Fancy fleeting like a bird,
You have Wealth and Fame, I've heard—
Those are things to be preferred."
He gave her both. The wealth she spent,
And then betrayed him, so Fame went.
But Love came not, in his despair;
She only smiled and left him there,
And he called her "The Woman Who Didn't Care,"
But the Devil cried, "You've had your share,
The game ends there.
Two of your wishes came through me,
But the Mighty Gods keep Number Three."

And the Gods grew stern as the Mills they turned,
That grind before they kill,
Till, staggering blind, with wandering mind,
And the glare of an imbecile,

From day to day he begs his way,
And whines his piteous call,
"The Mills of the Gods grind slowly,
Yet they grind exceeding small."

1. What three things did the man in the poem desire? Which of those three things eluded him?

2. Was he a lovable person? What was the cost of his ambition?

3. Choose six words to describe this man. He is:

4. Compare and contrast Ivy Elm's life with the life of the man in the poem.

5. Would you be willing to give up love and companionship for fortune and ambition?

6. Take a poll. Ask at least 10 of your peers if they would be willing to give up love and companionship for fortune and ambition. Then ask the same question to 10 people who are forty years old or older. Was there a difference by age? Did females respond differently than males?

Extra Credit

Write an essay, story or poem using this quotation as the theme:

> *Nothing is ever enough when what you are looking for isn't what you really want.*
>
> Arianna Stassinopoulos Huffington

Journal entry:
> Do you have a savings account? Is saving money impor-
> tant to you? Why do you suppose that saving money is
> important to many people?

The Savings Book

by Gary Soto

My wife, Carolyn, married me for my savings: Not the double digit figures but the strange three or four dollar withdrawals and deposits. The first time she saw my passbook she laughed until her eyes became moist and then hugged me as she called "Poor baby." And there was truth to what she was saying: Poor.

I remember opening my savings account at Guarantee Savings May 27, 1969, which was a Monday. The previous Saturday my brother and I had taken a labor bus to chop cotton in the fields west of Fresno. We returned home in the back of a pickup with fourteen dollars each and a Mexican national who kept showing us watches and rings for us to buy. That day my brother and I wouldn't spring for Cokes or sandwiches, as most everyone else on our crew did when a vending truck drove up at lunch time, tooting a loud horn. The driver opened the aluminum doors to display his goods, and the workers, who knew better but couldn't resist, hovered over the iced Cokes, the cellophaned sandwiches, and the Hostess cupcakes. We looked on from the shade of the bus, sullen and most certainly sensible. Why pay forty cents when you could get a Coke in town for half the price. Why buy a sandwich for sixty-five cents when you could have slapped together your own sandwich. That was what our mother had done for us. She had made us tuna sandwiches which by noon had grown suspiciously sour when we peeled back the top slice to peek in. Still, we ate them, chewing slowly and watching each other to see if he were beginning to double over. Finished, we searched the paper bag and found a broken stack of saltine crackers wrapped in wax paper. What a cruel mother, we thought. Dry crackers on a dry day when it was sure to rise into the nineties as we chopped cotton or, as the saying went, "played Mexican golf."

We had each earned fourteen dollars for eight hours of work, the most money I had ever made in one day. Two days later, on May 27, 1969, I deposited those dollars; on June 9th I made my first withdrawal—four dollars to buy a belt to match a pair of pants. I had just been hired to sell encyclopedias, and the belt was intended to dazzle my prospective clients when they opened the door to receive me. But in reality few welcomed my presence on their doorsteps and the only encyclopedias I sold that summer were to families on welfare who so desperately wanted to rise from their soiled lives. Buy a set, I told them, and your problems will disappear. Knowledge is power. Education is the key to the future, and so on. The contracts, however, were rescinded and my commissions with them.

On June 20 I withdrew three dollars and twenty-five cents to buy a plain white shirt because my boss had suggested that I should look more "professional." Still, I sold encyclopedias to the poor and again the contracts were thrown out. Finally I was fired, my briefcase taken away, and the company tie undone from my neck. I walked home in the summer heat despairing at the consequence: No new clothes for the fall.

On July 13 I took out five dollars and eighty cents which, including the five cents interest earned, left me with a balance of one dollar. I used the money for bus fare to Los Angeles to look for work. I found it in a tire factory. At summer's end I returned home and walked proudly to Guarantee Savings with my pockets stuffed with ten dollar bills. That was September 5, and my new balance jumped to one hundred and forty-one dollars. I was a senior in high school and any withdrawals from my account went exclusively to buy clothes, never for food, record albums, or concerts. On September 15, for instance, I withdrew fifteen dollars for a shirt and jeans. On September 24 I again stood before the teller to ask for six dollars. I bought a sweater at the Varsity Shop at Coffee's.

Slowly my savings dwindled that fall semester, although I did beef it up with small deposits: Twenty dollars on October 1, ten dollars on November 19, fifteen dollars on December 31, and so on. But by February my savings account balance read three dollars and twelve cents. On March 2 I returned to the bank to withdraw one crisp dollar to do God knows what. Perhaps it was to buy my mother a birthday gift. Seven days later, on March 10, I made one last attempt to bolster my savings by adding eight dollars. By March 23, however, I was again down to one dollar.

By the time I finally closed my account, it had fluctuated for five years, rising and falling as a barometer to my financial quandary. What is curious to me about this personal history are the kinds of transactions that took place—one day I would withdraw three dollars while on another day I would ask for six. How did it vanish? What did it buy? I'm almost certain I bought clothes but for what occasion? For whom? I didn't have a girlfriend in my senior year, so where did the money go?

To withdraw those minor amounts was no easy task. I had to walk or bicycle nearly four miles, my good friend Scott tagging along, and afterward we'd walk up and down the Fresno Mall in search of the elusive girlfriend or, if worse came to worst, to look for trouble.

My savings book is a testimony to my fear of poverty—that by saving a dollar here, another there, it would be kept at bay.

I admit that as a kid I worried about starving, although there was probably no reason. There was always something to eat; the cupboards were weighed down with boxes of this and that. But when I was older the remembrance of difficult times stayed with me: The time Mother was picking grapes and my brother ate our entire lunch while my sister and I played under the vines. For us there was nothing to eat that day. The time I opened the refrigerator at my father's (who was separated from our mother at the time) to stare at one puckered apple that sat in the conspicuous glare of the refrigerator's light. I recalled my uncle lying on a couch dying of cancer. I recalled my father who died from an accident a year later and left us in even more roughed up shoes. I had not been born to be scared out of my wits, but that is what happened. Through a set of experiences early in my life, I grew up fearful that some financial tragedy would strike at any moment, as when I was certain that the recession of 1973 would lead to chaos—burned cars and street fighting. During the recession I roomed with my brother and I suggested that we try to become vegetarians. My brother looked up from his drawing board and replied: "Aren't we already?" I thought about it for a while, and it was true. I was getting most of my hearty meals from my girlfriend, Carolyn, who would later become my wife. She had a job with great pay, and when she opened her refrigerator I almost wept for the bologna, sliced ham, and drumsticks. I spied the cheeses and imported olives, tomatoes, and the artichoke hearts. I opened the freezer—chocolate ice cream!

At that time Carolyn put up with my antics, so when I suggested that we buy fifty dollars worth of peanut butter and pinto beans to store under her bed, she happily wrote out a check because she was in love and didn't know any better. I was certain that in 1974 the country would slide into a depression and those who were not prepared would be lost. We hid the rations in the house and sat at the front window to wait for something to happen.

What happened was that we married and I loosened up. I still fear the worst, but the worst is not what it once was. Today I bought a pair of shoes; tomorrow I may splurge to see a movie, with a box of popcorn and a large soda that will wash it all down. It's time to live, I tell myself, and if a five dollar bill flutters from my hands, no harm will result. I laugh at the funny scenes that aren't funny, and I can't think of any better life.

---

1. Gary Soto said, "My savings book is a testimony to my fear of poverty." Do you fear poverty?

2. Review the activity on page 103 of *Career Choices*. Make a list of some of the ways that you can avoid becoming a poverty statistic. Evaluate your list and circle the top two strategies you've generated to avoid poverty. Was one of those top strategies having a substantial savings account?

3. Stories like "The Savings Book" usually remind us of our grandparent's comments about living in the depression. Can Soto's story be applied to poverty in the 80's? the 90's? What are the similarities between Soto's experience and poverty today? What are the contrasts?

Writing Activity

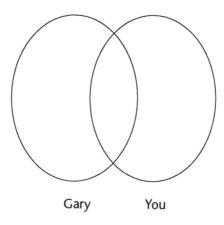

Gary   You

Venn Diagram

What did you learn from the story about Gary's personality? Re-examine the text and look for descriptions that would provide you with information about his character. How are you similar to Gary? How are you different? Complete a Venn Diagram for Gary and yourself. First, think about how you and the character are different. Fill in the differences in the outside spaces of the diagram, Gary's characteristics are on one side and yours are on the other. Then, determine what you have in common with his character and fill in the center of the diagram with these qualities. Use the information you've generated on the Venn Diagram to help you address the following prompt:

In literature, we read about many characters who remind us of ourselves, our values, our ideas, the problems that we encounter in life and the joys that we experience. Write a fully developed paragraph in which you compare and contrast the qualities that Gary has to the ones that you recognize in your own personality.

Menu: Choose One of the Following Activities

A. INDIVIDUAL: Gary has become a copywriter for the Fresno Creative Services. He has been asked to write a thirty second radio commercial for City Savings and Loan which encourages people to save money. Create the copy for this advertisement.

GROUP: Most ad copy is not created by one person. Form a creative committee of two or three peers and brainstorm, write, edit and fine tune your copy.

B. Assume that twenty years from now you are taking your ten year old daughter to the bank to open her first savings account. What will you say to her about saving money? What questions will she ask and how will you respond? Create that conversation.

C. Financial planners recommend that people reserve at least
    25% of their annual earnings in a savings account. Do
    you agree or disagree with this advice? List all of the
    reasons that you should save this amount. Evaluate your
    reasons and write a statement reflecting your philosophy
    about saving money.

Gary Soto 1952–

Gary Soto writes about growing up Hispanic in
California's Central Valley. This story is from *Living
Up the Street* (1985), a volume of short stories.
Soto finds in the smallest childhood incidents the
occasion for literature. His style is described as
being poetic and his first book of poetry *The Elements of San Joaquin,* reflects his careful, intense
attention to language. His latest work, *A Summer
Life,* is a collection of thirty nine essays. He is an
instructor at U.C. Berkeley.

Journal entry:
> The plight of the homeless has received a lot of attention in the last several years. What do you think when you see people living on the streets and in the public areas of our communities? Explain what you think and how you feel when you see people who are homeless.

Miss Rosie

by Lucille Clifton

When I watch you
wrapped up like garbage
sitting, surrounded by the smell
of too old potato peels
or
when I watch you
in your old man's shoes
with the little toe cut out
sitting, waiting for your mind
like next week's grocery
I say
When I watch you
you wet brown bag of a woman
who used to be the best looking gal in Georgia
used to be called the Georgia Rose
I stand up
through your destruction
I stand up

1. Lucille Clifton uses sensory images to paint a portrait of Rosie. What do you see? What do you smell? Choose a vivid image in this poem to depict in a drawing. How do you see Miss Rosie?

2. What similes can you find in this poem? What metaphors are used?

3. What could Lucille Clifton have meant when she wrote:

   "I stand up
   through your destruction
   I stand up"

   What is her destruction? Why does the narrator say that she will "stand up" to Miss Rosie's destruction?

4. Think about Miss Rosie's life. What might she have been like when she was 15 years old? What were her priorities? What was she doing with her life? What were her plans for the future?

5. As a class, brainstorm the causes of homelessness. How does this happen? Can you imagine being without resources, or the support of family or friends who could help you, to the point where you could no longer afford a place to live or food to eat? Two possibilities are:

   You become seriously ill. You do not have medical insurance, and you lose your job.

   You have two children, ages two and four. You are now single and have custody of the children. You have only minimum employment skills and cannot earn enough to pay for childcare.

   On the board list a variety of situations which could lead to homelessness. After discussing, review the list of circumstances generated by members of the class. Choose one of these scenarios and write a fictional account of a typical day in the life of a homeless person. Use the first person narrative form.

Lucille Clifton 1936–

Lucille Clifton was born in Depew, New York. She has written books for children and poetry for adults. The author of *The Black ABC's*, and *Good News About the Earth*, her book of poetry, *An Ordinary Woman* and "Miss Rosie," reflect Clifton's compassion for the people and events of everyday life. Lucille Clifton won a National Endowment for the Arts award in 1970 and 1972 and she is the poet-in-residence at Coppin State College in Baltimore, Maryland where she lives.

Journal entry:
> Imagine that you are a single parent who is unemployed, you have depleted your available cash, and will have no money coming in for another week. You have very little food in the house, and your five year old child suddenly becomes ill and needs medical attention. What options do you have? How do you feel? Jot down a list of words that describe how you would feel if you were in this situation.

Christmas Day in the Workhouse

by George R. Sims

It is Christmas Day in the workhouse, and the cold, bare walls are bright
With garlands of green and holly, and the place is a pleasant sight;
For with clean-washed hands and faces in a long and hungry line
The paupers sit at the table, for this is the hour they dine.

And the guardians and their ladies, although the wind is east,
Have come in their furs and wrappers to watch their charges feast;
To smile and be condescending, putting on pauper plates.
To be hosts at the workhouse banquet they've paid for—with the rates.

O, the paupers are meek and lowly with their "Thank'ee kindly, mums!"
So long as they fill their stomachs what matter it whence it comes?
But one of the old men mutters and pushes his plate aside,
"Great God!" he cries, "but it chokes me; for this is the day she died!"

The guardians gazed in horror, the master's face went white;
"Did a pauper refuse their pudding? Could that their ears believe aright?"
Then the ladies clutched their husbands, thinking the man would die,
Struck by a bolt, or something, by the outraged One on high.

But the pauper sat for a moment, then rose 'mid silence grim,
For the others had ceased to chatter and trembled in every limb:
He looked at the guardians' ladies, then, eyeing their lords, he said;
"I eat not the food of villains whose hands are foul and red;

"Whose victims cry for vengeance from their dark, unhallowed graves."
"He's drunk," said the workhouse master, "or else he's mad and raves."
"Not drunk or mad," cried the pauper, "but only a haunted beast,
Who, torn by the hounds and mangled, declines the vulture's feast.

"I care not a curse for the guardians, and I won't be dragged away;
Just let me have the fit out, it's only on Christmas Day
That the black past comes to goad me and prey on my burning brain;
I'll tell you the rest in a whisper—I swear I won't shout again.

"Keep your hands off me, curse you! Hear me right out to the end.
You come here to see how paupers the season of Christmas spend;
You come here to watch us feeding, as they watched the captured beast;
Here's why a penniless pauper spits on your paltry feast.

"Do you think I will take your bounty and let you smile and think
You're doing a noble action with the parish's meat and drink?
Where is my wife, you traitors—the poor old wife you slew?
Yes, by the God above me, my Nance was killed by you.

"Last Winter my wife lay dying, starved in a filthy den.
I had never been to the parish—I came to the parish then;
I swallowed my pride in coming! for ere the ruin came
I held up my head as a trader, and I bore a spotless name.

"I came to the parish, craving bread for a starving wife—
Bread for the woman who'd loved me thro' fifty years of life;
And what do you think they told me, mocking my awful grief,
That the house was open to us, but they wouldn't give out relief.

"I slunk to the filthy alley—'twas a cold, raw Christmas Eve—
And the bakers' shops were open, tempting a man to thieve;
But I clenched my fists together, holding my head awry,
So I came to her empty-handed and mournfully told her why.

Continued

"Then I told her the house was open; she had heard of the ways of that
For her bloodless cheeks went crimson, and up in her rags she sat,
Crying, 'Bide the Christmas here, John, we've never had one apart;
I think I can bear the hunger—the other would break my heart.'

"All through that eve I watched her, holding her hand in mine,
Praying the Lord and weeping till my lips were salt as brine;

I asked her once if she hungered, and she answered 'No.'
The moon shone in at the window, set in a wreath of snow.

"Then the room was bathed in glory, and I saw in my darling's eyes
The faraway look of wonder that comes when the spirit flies;
And her lips were parched and parted, and her reason came and went.
For she rav'd of our home in Devon, where our happiest years were spent.

"And the accents, long forgotten, came back to the tongue once more.
For she talked like the country lassie I woo'd by the Devon shore;
Then she rose to her feet and trembled, and fell on the rags and moaned,
And, 'Give me a crust—I'm famished—for the love of God,' she groaned.

"I rushed from the room like a madman and flew to the workhouse gate,
Crying, 'Food for a dying woman!' and the answer came, 'Too late;'
They drove me away with curses; then I fought with a dog in the street
And tore from the mongrel's clutches a crust he was trying to eat.

"Back through the filthy byways! Back through the trampled slush!
Up to the crazy garret, wrapped in an awful hush;
My heart sank down at the threshold, and I paused with a sudden thrill,
For there, in the silv'ry moonlight, my Nance lay cold and still.

"Up to the blackened ceiling the sunken eyes were cast—
I knew on those lips, all bloodless, my name had been the last;
She called for her absent husband—O God! Had I known—
Had called in vain, and, in anguish, had died in that den alone.

"Yes, there in a land of plenty, lay a loving woman dead.
Cruelly starved and murdered for a loaf of the parish bread;
At yonder gate, last Christmas, I craved for a human life,
You, who would feed us paupers, what of my murdered wife?

"There, get ye gone to your dinners, don't mind me in the least;
Think of the happy paupers eating your Christmas feast;
And when you recount their blessings in your parochial way,
Say what you did for me, too, only last Christmas Day."

---

1. As soon as you've read the poem, make a list of adjectives that describe the feelings that reading the poem evoked. Compare this list with the words that you wrote down before reading the poem. Are any of the words on both lists? Are any words different? Which list is more complete?

2. How successful was the author in causing you to react emotionally to the issue of poverty and helplessness?

3. Think about the guardian, the workhouse master and the pauper. Ponder the status of each of these people. What level of education do you think each of these people attained? Compare your ideas with another student; were your ideas about the level of education for each character similar or different?

4. Now, imagine each of these characters at age seventeen. From this character's point of view, write a paragraph to describe what each person was doing at age seventeen. Think about how you can incorporate ways to show the status of the character that you have chosen.

5. Pretend that you are one of the workhouse guardians, perhaps president of the board of directors. An exposé of this story makes the headlines of a major metropolitan newspaper. Write a letter to the editor justifying your actions. Think about how you can present your case and try to persuade the readers that you were right to turn the pauper away.

Narrative Poems

"Christmas Day in the Workhouse" is an example of narrative poetry. It is a poem that tells a story.

Journal entry:
> Why do we give gifts to people who are important to us?
> How much are you willing to sacrifice to make someone
> you care about happy?

The Gift of the Magi

by O. Henry

One dollar and eighty-seven cents. That was all. And sixty cents of it was in pennies. Pennies saved one and two at a time by bulldozing the grocer and the vegetable man and the butcher until one's cheeks burned with the silent imputation of parsimony that such close dealing implied. Three times Della counted it. One dollar and eighty-seven cents. And the next day would be Christmas.

There was clearly nothing to do but flop down on the shabby little couch and howl. So Della did it. Which instigates the moral reflection that life is made up of sobs, sniffles, and smiles, with sniffles predominating.

While the mistress of the home is gradually subsiding from the first stage to the second, take a look at the home. A furnished flat at $8 per week. It did not exactly beggar description, but it certainly had that word on the lookout for the mendicancy squad.

In the vestibule below was a letter-box into which no letter would go, and an electric button from which no mortal finger could coax a ring. Also appertaining thereunto was a card bearing the name "Mr. James Dillingham Young."

The "Dillingham" had been flung to the breeze during a former period of prosperity when its possessor was being paid

$30 per week. Now, when the income was shrunk to $20, the letters of "Dillingham" looked blurred, as though they were thinking seriously of contracting to a modest and unassuming D. But whenever Mr. James Dillingham Young came home and reached his flat above he was called "Jim" and greatly hugged by Mrs. James Dillingham Young, already introduced to you as Della. Which is all very good.

Della finished her cry and attended to her cheeks with the powder rag. She stood by the window and looked out dully at a gray cat walking a gray fence in a gray backyard. Tomorrow would be Christmas Day, and she had only $1.87 with which to buy Jim a present. She had been saving every penny she could for months, with this result. Twenty dollars a week doesn't go far. Expenses had been greater than she had calculated. They always are. Only $1.87 to buy a present for Jim. Her Jim. Many a happy hour she had spent planning for something nice for him. Something fine and rare and sterling—something just a little bit near to being worthy of the honor of being owned by Jim.

There was a pier glass between the windows of the room. Perhaps you have seen a pier glass in an $8 flat. A very thin and very agile person may, by observing his reflection in a rapid sequence of longitudinal strips, obtain a fairly accurate conception of his looks. Della, being slender, had mastered the art.

Suddenly she whirled from the window and stood before the glass. Her eyes were shining brilliantly, but her face had lost its color within twenty seconds. Rapidly she pulled down her hair and let it fall to its full length.

Now, there were two possessions of the James Dillingham Youngs in which they both took a mighty pride. One was Jim's gold watch that had been his father's and his grandfather's. The other was Della's hair. Had the Queen of Sheba lived in the flat across the airshaft, Della would have let her hair hang out the window some day to dry just to depreciate Her Majesty's jewels and gifts. Had King Solomon been the janitor, with all his treasures piled up in the basement, Jim would have pulled out his watch every time he passed, just to see him pluck at his beard from envy.

So now Della's beautiful hair fell about her rippling and shining like a cascade of brown waters. It reached below her knee and made itself almost a garment for her. And then she did it up again nervously and quickly. Once she faltered for a minute and stood still while a tear or two splashed on the worn red carpet.

On went her old brown jacket; on went her old brown hat. With a whirl of skirts and with the brilliant sparkle still in her eyes, she fluttered out the door and down the stairs to the street.

Where she stopped the sign read: "Mme. Sofronie. Hair Goods of All Kinds." One flight up Della ran, and collected herself, panting. Madame, large, too white, chilly, hardly looked the "Sofronie."

"Will you buy my hair?" asked Della.

"I buy hair," said Madame. "Take your hat off and let's have a sight at the looks of it."

Down rippled the brown cascade.

"Twenty dollars." said Madame, lifting the mass with a practiced hand.

"Give it to me quick." said Della.

Oh, and the next two hours tripped by on rosy wings. Forget the hashed metaphor. She was ransacking the stores for Jim's present.

She found it at last. It surely had been made for Jim and no one else. There was no other like it in any of the stores, and she had turned all of them inside out. It was a platinum fob chain simple and chaste in design, properly proclaiming its value by substance alone and not by meretricious ornamentation—as all good things should do. It was even worthy of The Watch. As soon as she saw it she knew that it must be Jim's. It was like him. Quietness and value—the description applied to both. Twenty-one dollars they took from her for it, and she hurried home with the 87 cents. With that chain on his watch Jim might be properly anxious about the time in any company. Grand as the watch was he sometimes looked at it on the sly on account of the old leather strap that he used in place of a chain.

When Della reached home her intoxication gave way a little to prudence and reason. She got out her curling irons and lighted the gas and went to work repairing the ravages made by generosity added to love. Which is always a tremendous task, dear friends—a mammoth task.

Within forty minutes her head was covered with tiny, close-lying curls that made her look wonderfully like a truant schoolboy. She looked at her reflection in the mirror long, carefully, and critically.

"If Jim doesn't kill me," she said to herself, "before he takes a second look at me, he'll say I look like a Coney Island chorus girl. But what could I do—oh! what could I do with a dollar and eighty-seven cents?"

At 7 o'clock the coffee was made and the frying-pan was on the back of the stove hot and ready to cook the chops.

Jim was never late. Della doubled the fob chain in her hand and sat on the corner of the table near the door that he always entered. Then she heard his step on the stair away down on the first flight, and she turned white for just a moment. She had a habit of saying little silent prayers about the simplest everyday things, and now she whispered: "Please God, make him think I am still pretty."

The door opened and Jim stepped in and closed it. He looked thin and very serious. Poor fellow, he was only twenty-two—and to be burdened with a family! He needed a new overcoat and he was without gloves.

Jim stopped inside the door, as immovable as a setter at the scent of quail. His eyes were fixed upon Della, and there was an expression in them that she could not read, and it terrified her. It was not anger, nor surprise, nor disapproval, nor horror, nor any of the sentiments that she had been prepared for. He simply stared at her fixedly with that peculiar expression on his face.

Della wriggled off the table and went for him.

"Jim, darling," she cried, "don't look at me that way. I had my hair cut off and sold it because I couldn't have lived through Christmas without giving you a present. It'll grow out again—you won't mind, will you? I just had to do it. My hair grows awfully fast. Say 'Merry Christmas!' Jim, and let's be happy. You don't know what a nice—what a beautiful, nice gift I've got for you."

"You've cut off your hair?" asked Jim, laboriously, as if he had not arrived at that patent fact yet even after the hardest mental labor.

"Cut it off and sold it," said Della. "Don't you like me just as well, anyhow? I'm me without my hair, ain't I?"

Jim looked about the room curiously.

"You say your hair is gone?" he said, with an air almost of idiocy.

"You needn't look for it," said Della. "It's sold, I tell you—sold and gone, too. It's Christmas Eve, boy. Be good to me, for it went for you. Maybe the hairs of my head were numbered," she went on with a sudden serious sweetness, "but nobody could ever count my love for you. Shall I put the chops on, Jim?"

Out of his trance Jim seemed quickly to wake. He enfolded his Della. For ten seconds let us regard with discreet scrutiny some inconsequential object in the other direction. Eight dollars a week or a million a year—what is the difference? A mathematician or a wit would give you the wrong answer. The Magi brought valuable gifts, but that was not among them. This dark assertion will be illuminated later on.

Jim drew a package from his overcoat pocket and threw it upon the table.

"Don't make any mistake, Dell," he said, "about me. I don't think there's anything in the way of a haircut or a shave or a shampoo that could make me like my girl any less. But if you'll unwrap that package you may see why you had me going a while at first."

White fingers and nimble tore at the string and paper. And then an ecstatic scream of joy; and then, alas! a quick feminine change to hysterical tears and wails, necessitating the immediate employment of all the comforting powers of the lord of the flat.

For there lay The Combs—the set of combs, side and back, that Della had worshipped for long in a Broadway window. Beautiful combs, pure tortoise shell, with jeweled rims—just the shade to wear in the beautiful vanished hair. They were expensive combs, she knew, and her heart had simply craved and yearned over them without the least hope of possession. And now, they were hers, but the tresses that should have adorned the coveted adornments were gone.

But she hugged them to her bosom, and at length she was able to look up with dim eyes and a smile and say: "My hair grows so fast, Jim!"

And then Della leaped up like a little singed cat and cried, "Oh, oh!"

Jim had not yet seen his beautiful present. She held it out to him eagerly upon her open palm. The dull precious metal seemed to flash with a reflection of her bright and ardent spirit.

"Isn't it a dandy, Jim? I hunted all over town to find it. You'll have to look at the time a hundred times a day now. Give me your watch. I want to see how it looks on it."

Instead of obeying, Jim tumbled down on the couch and put his hands under the back of his head and smiled.

"Dell," said he, "let's put our Christmas presents away and keep 'em a while. They're too nice to use just at present. I sold the watch to get the money to buy your combs. And now suppose you put the chops on."

The Magi, as you know, were wise men—wonderfully wise men—who brought gifts to the Babe in the manger. They invented the art of giving Christmas presents. Being wise, their gifts were no doubt wise ones, possibly bearing the privilege of exchange in case of duplication. And here I have lamely related to you the uneventful chronicle of two foolish children in a flat who most unwisely sacrificed for each other the greatest treasures of their house. But in a last word to the wise of these days let it be said that of all who give gifts these two were the wisest. Of all who give and receive gifts, such as they are wisest. Everywhere they are wisest. They are the magi.

---

1. Early in the action of the story, O. Henry shows us what possessions Jim and Della value most; what are they?
2. How does Della afford to buy Jim's gift?
3. Why is Jim sorry that Della has lost her hair? How does Jim feel when he opens Della's gift?
4. Explain the following: "Of all who give and receive gifts, such as they are wisest." What is O. Henry saying about the characters in this story?

Creative Writing

O. Henry was famous for the surprise endings to his stories. This story is clearly about another era, a world where long hair could be sold for money and men wore watch fobs that fit into a special pocket on their vests. The genuine feelings that these two people had for each other, however, are ageless. People still are committed to each other and willing to sacrifice to make the other person happy. Use O. Henry's plot as the basis for a 90's story. What would Jim and Della sacrifice in this day and age to make each other happy? Have fun with this one and don't forget the plot-twist at the end of your story.

O. Henry 1862–1910

O. Henry (William Sidney Porter) lived from 1862-1910. At the age of eighteen, William Porter moved from North Carolina to Texas. He worked in Texas as a ranch hand, a bank teller, and a newspaper reporter. During this time, he was indicted for embezzling funds from the bank, and he fled to Central America. He later returned to the United States to see his dying wife. He was arrested, tried, convicted, and sent to prison. During his three and a half year sentence, he served as the prison pharmacist and began writing short stories under pseudonyms. He finally chose the name O. Henry. After his release, Porter went to New York and wrote several short story collections including *Cabbages and Kings*, *The Four Million*, and *The Trimmed Lamp*.

Journal entry:
> When was the last time you made a commitment to something or someone? Describe that situation. What does the word commitment mean to you? How important is it to you?

A Legacy for My Daughter
by James Webb

Newsweek Magazine, November 7, 1988

On the dresser in her empty bedroom was a yellow music box with Snoopy on the lid. It had been a gift to her when she was four or five. She had outgrown it years before, and yet could never bear to part with it. It connected her to simpler days and, although its melody was seldom heard in the house now, the music box remained.

I picked it up the evening after my daughter Amy departed for college. In the space of a few hours, her bedroom seemed like a museum. It haunted me with its silence, its unaccustomed tidiness; with the odd souvenirs from a childhood that was now history. But it was the music box that caught my eye. I opened it and the plaintive song that recalled her years of innocence played automatically, surprising me, as I remembered, tears filling my eyes, the small child holding the box before she went to sleep. When I saw that she had placed my Marine Corps ribbons from Vietnam inside, I wept like a fool.

I had not seen the ribbons in 10 years. When she was very small, she would wear them to school, picking out one or a few to match a jacket or a sweater. It perplexed her mother and caused her teacher to think I was a militarist at a time when virulent antimilitarism was *de rigueur*. But she had asked me for them and had worn them as an act of faith because even at five she could read inside my heart. She had conceived a way, as if we shared a secret pact, to show her loyalty on an issue that was drowning me in pain.

At a time when life had closed in on me, when right and wrong had canceled each other out, when the country was in chaos and I was struggling with the wreckage of my life, my daughter was my friend. At three, she comforted me, asking the right questions when I learned that my closest friend in law school had died. At five, she tried to take care of me when, badly shaken by the suicide of a young veteran I had tried to help—he had been unfairly convicted of murder in Vietnam—I retreated to a remote campsite. Wherever I went, Amy came with me. She learned about bars and pool halls and became a pinball wizard by the time she was seven. At 10, as her class cheered the return of our hostages from Iran, she lectured them on the difficult homecoming of our Vietnam veterans.

It occurred to me, sitting in her bedroom, that the incubator had hatched and that I had just delivered an adult into the world as surely as her mother had delivered an infant 18 years before. These childhood years have formed her view of the world, but like so many of her compatriots, her life echoed with the turmoil of her elders.

Amy grew up listening to the disagreements of her parents, both before and after their divorce. She learned what it meant to be a "latchkey kid," cared for by phone. She heard those who celebrated the drug culture tell her "just say no" at about the same time that high-school dealers started wearing beepers to class. She knows that the generation that flaunted sexual freedom is queasy now, what with abortion so common among teenagers and their illegitimacy rate triple that of 20 years ago.

Mine has not been a generation that offered its children certainties. We have treated them to endless argument instead.

Throughout her young life, my daughter has been treated to a view that government is corrupt and unfair, this was fed by continuous debates over civil rights, the Vietnam War, Watergate and the Iran-contra affair. She has also watched the nation blunder about in its role as world leader, jerked this way and that on foreign-policy issues and by leaders who appear to be selling her future to foreign investors instead of calling on citizens to regain the self-discipline that made us great.

Grand debate: I fear that the greatest legacy of the baby-boom generation will be that although it asked all the right questions in the early years of its adulthood, it resolved nothing. Raised by parents whose sacrifices during the Great Depression and World War War II purchased for us the luxury of being able to question, we all understood the standards from which some of us were choosing to deviate. But lacking unity, riven by disagreement on every major issue and most minor ones, we have, perhaps unwittingly, encouraged our children to believe that there are no touch stones, no true answers, no commitments worthy of sacrifice. Our children have been treated to grand debate and in many cases have grown up under the false illusion that there are no firm principles. That for every cause there is a countercause. For every reason to fight there is a reason to run. For every yin there is a yang.

How will our children react to this philosophical quagmire, this unbecoming hesitance which, ironically, is the product not of our cynicism but of our idealism, once they learn more clearly their own place in the flow of history? My bet is that they will surprise us with their stability, that they will perhaps be slower to make commitments, but more serious when they do. Someone who has bounced between two parents will not marry with the thought that "we can always get a divorce if it doesn't work." Someone who has viewed the nightmarish results of political policies and recreational activities that were rather innocently begun will be more careful to consider the implications of new seductions at the outset.

In the end, just as my tiny daughter-friend eased my personal turmoil years ago, she and her contemporaries may in time become the philosophical arbiters of the generation that spawned them. How poetic, to think that those who were denied certainties in their childhood might in turn bring some synthesis to their parents.

Thinking of these things as I sat in the quiet of a bedroom gone empty after my beautiful sweet friend's flight to adulthood, listening to the yellow music box that still reminds me of the adoration in Amy's eyes, I then understood another truth: that we, the members of a creative, sometimes absurd, always narcissistic postwar generation, will soon receive a judgment. Whatever it is, our children have earned the right to make it.

---

1. Re-read the first two paragraphs of this essay. What is especially effective about the way that the topic is introduced? How did Webb skillfully lead the reader into the subject?

2. What details are provided to portray the relationship between the father and his daughter? List the details and explain their significance.

3. What were some of the problems that James Webb struggled with in his life?

4. How is Webb's generation described in paragraphs seven and eight?

5. What does he think will be different about the values of Amy's generation?

6. Interview your parent or guardian about a situation where they felt they succeeded or failed. What did you learn from their experience?

7. Finish the statement, and make it into a topic sentence for a short paragraph: "If I ever have children, I hope they will value . . .":

8. In a well developed essay, discuss the "legacy" you hope your generation leaves to their children.

James Webb 1946–

James Webb is an Annapolis graduate, a Vietnam war hero who was severely wounded, a lawyer, and a Pulitzer prize winner for *Fields of Fire*, a fictionalized account of his Vietnam experience. He was a Secretary of the Navy during the Reagan administration and he resigned to protest the cutting of the Navy fleets below six hundred ships.

Journal entry:
> Have you ever considered entering a profession that requires a great deal of writing? Why do you think people become professional writers?
>
> Define the following words based on your idea of what they mean:
>> endure
>> prevail
>
> Now, check the dictionary to clarify your understanding of the meaning of the two words.

I Decline to Accept the End of Man
by William Faulkner

Stockholm, December 10, 1950

I feel that this award was not made to me as a man but to my work—a life's work in the agony and sweat of the human spirit, not for glory and least of all for profit, but to create out of the materials of the human spirit something which did not exist before. So this award is only mine in trust. It will not be difficult to find a dedication for the money part of it commensurate with the purpose and significance of its origin. But I would like to do the same with the acclaim too, by using this moment as a pinnacle from which I might be listened to by the young men and women already dedicated to the same anguish and travail, among whom is already that one who will some day stand here where I am standing.

Our tragedy today is a general and universal physical fear so long sustained by now that we can even bear it. There are no longer problems of the spirit. There is only the question:

When will I be blown up? Because of this, the young man or woman writing today has forgotten the problems of the human heart in conflict with itself which alone can make good writing because only that is worth writing about, worth the agony and the sweat.

He must learn them again. He must teach himself that the basest of all things is to be afraid; and, teaching himself that, forget it forever, leaving no room in his workshop for anything but the old verities and truths of the heart, the old universal truths lacking which any story is ephemeral and doomed—love and honor and pity and pride and compassion and sacrifice. Until he does so, he labors under a curse. He writes not of love but of lust, of defeats in which nobody loses anything of value, of victories without hope and, worst of all, without pity or compassion. His griefs grieve on no universal bones, leaving no scars. He writes not of the heart but of the glands.

Until he relearns these things, he will write as though he stood alone and watched the end of man. I decline to accept the end of man. It is easy enough to say that man is immortal simply because he will endure; that when the last ding-dong of doom has clanged and faded from the last worthless rock hanging tideless in the last red and dying evening, that even then there will still be one more sound: that of his puny inexhaustible voice, still talking. I refuse to accept this. I believe that man will not merely endure: he will prevail. He is immortal, not because he alone among creatures has an inexhaustible voice but because he has a soul, a spirit capable of compassion and sacrifice and endurance. The poet's, the writer's, duty is to write about these things. It is his privilege to help man endure by lifting his heart, by reminding him of the courage and honor and hope and pride and compassion and pity and sacrifice which have been the glory of his past. The poet's voice need not merely be the record of man, it can be one of the props, the pillars to help him endure and prevail.

1. How does Faulkner define good writing?
2. What was the "tragedy today" referred to in paragraph two?
3. What does Faulkner believe to be the "basest of all things"?
4. What makes man immortal?
5. What is the poet's and the writer's duty?
6. What are the "old universal truths"?
7. What does he mean when he states: "The poet's voice need not merely be the record of man, it can be one of the props, the pillars to help him endure and prevail"?
8. Choose one of the quotations below and develop an essay on that theme.

> *Writers give people beliefs, and giving people beliefs helps change history.*
> Norman Cousins

> *Writers are mirrors of the era in which they live.*
> Lin Ying

> *I am part of all that I have read.*
> John Kiern

9. List five to ten careers for people who love to write.
10. Faulkner states that the next prize winner might be a young man or woman in his listening audience. Based on evidence in his speech, do you think he really believed that the next winner would be female? Do some research, who have been the female Nobel prize winners in the field of literature?

Art Activity

The following activity will require colored construction paper, pastels, tissue and felt pens.

Choose your favorite line or lines from this speech. Write the lines in your best writing on a large, light colored sheet of construction paper. Then, tear several strips of construction paper. Use pastels to coat the torn edge of a strip of paper. Transfer the color onto your large sheet (with the quotation) by rubbing it off with the tissue. The process of rubbing the pastel from the torn edge will produce some interesting patterns. You can use a variety of colors and make it abstract or make a design like a sunset, or a mountain range. The finished results will make a great bulletin board display.

William Faulkner 1897–1962

William Faulkner, the American author, was fifty-three at the time he delivered this speech in Stockholm, Sweden, on December 10, 1950. He reiterated his faith in man's eternal dominion over destiny as he accepted the Nobel Prize for Literature. His speech is considered one of the shortest but finest acceptance speeches. *The Sound and the Fury* and *As I Lay Dying* are among his best known novels. He wrote many other short stories, novels and essays, as well, and is considered by many people to be America's greatest writer. Faulkner's readership was limited in the United States, but he was a best selling author in Western Europe in the post-war years.

Journal entry:
> As a child, did you ever want to run away and join the circus? What is your current ambition; has it changed since you were a child?
>
> Knowing the meaning of the following words will make your reading of "A Boy's Ambition" more enjoyable:
>
> transient, eminence, exalted, obscurity, contentment, tranquil, disconsolate

from *Life on the Mississippi*

by Mark Twain

The Boys' Ambition

When I was a boy, there was but one permanent ambition among my comrades in our village on the west bank of the Mississippi River. That was, to be a steamboatman. We had transient ambitions of other sorts, but they were only transient.

When a circus came and went, it left us all burning to become clowns; the first Negro minstrel show that came to our section left us all suffering to try that kind of life; now and then we had a hope that if we lived and were good, God would permit us to be pirates. These ambitions faded out, each in its turn; but the ambition to be a steamboatman always remained.

Once a day a cheap, gaudy packet arrived upward from St. Louis, and another downward from Keokuk. Before these events, the day was glorious with expectancy; after them, the day was a dead and empty thing. Not only the boys, but the whole village, felt this. After all these years I can picture that old time to myself now, just as it was then: the white town drowsing in the sunshine of a summer's morning; the streets empty, or pretty nearly so; one or two clerks sitting in front of the Water Street stores, with their splint-bottomed chairs tilted back against the wall, chins on breasts, hats slouched over their faces, asleep—with shingle shavings enough around to show what broke them down; a sow and a litter of pigs loafing along the sidewalk, doing a good business in watermelon rinds and seeds; two or three lonely little freight piles scattered about the levee; a pile of skids on the slope of the stone-paved wharf, and the fragrant town drunkard asleep in the shadow of them; two or three wood flats at the head of the wharf, but nobody to listen to the peaceful lapping of the wavelets against them; the great Mississippi the majestic, the magnificent Mississippi rolling its mile-wide tide along, shining in the sun; the dense forest away on the other side; the point above the town, and the point below, bounding the river–glimpse and turning it into a sort of sea, and withal a very still and brilliant and lonely one. Presently a film of dark smoke appears above one of those remote points; instantly a Negro drayman, famous for his quick eye and prodigious voice lifts up the cry, "S-t-e-a-m-boat a-comin," and the scene changes! The town drunkard stirs, the clerks wake up, a furious clatter of drays follows, every house and store pours out a human contribution, and all in a twinkling the dead town is alive and moving. Drays, carts, men, boys, all go hurrying from many quarters to a common center, the wharf. Assembled there, the people fasten their eyes upon the coming boat as upon a wonder they are seeing for the first time. And the boat *is* rather a handsome sight, too. She is long and sharp and trim and pretty; she has two tall, fancy-topped chimneys, with a gilded device of some kind strung between them; a fanciful pilothouse, all glass and gingerbread, perched on top of the texas deck behind them; the paddleboxes are gorgeous with a picture or with gilded rays above the boat's name; the boiler deck, the hurricane deck, and the texas deck are fenced and ornamented with clean white railings; there is a flag gallantly flying from the jackstaff; the furnace doors are open and the fires glaring bravely; the upper decks are black with passengers; the captain stands by the big bell, calm, imposing, the envy of all; great volumes of the blackest smoke are rolling and tumbling out of the chimneys—a husbanded grandeur created with a bit of pitch pine just before arriving at a town; the crew are grouped on the forecastle; the broad stage is run far out over the port bow, and an envied deckhand stands picturesquely on the end of it with a coil of rope in his hand; the pent steam is screaming through the gauge cocks; the captain lifts his hand, a bell rings, the wheels stop, then they turn back, churning the water to foam, and the steamer is at rest. Then such a scramble as there is to get aboard, and to get ashore, and to take in freight and to discharge freight, all at one and the same time; and such a yelling and cursing as the mates facilitate it all with. Ten minutes later the steamer is under way again, with no flag on the jackstaff and no black smoke issuing from the chimneys. After ten more minutes the town is dead again, and the town drunkard asleep by the skids once more.

My father was a justice of the peace, and I supposed he possessed the power of life and death over all men and could hang anybody that offended him. This was distinction enough for me as a general thing; but the desire to be a steamboatman kept intruding, nevertheless. I first wanted to be a cabin boy, so that I could come out with a white apron on and shake a tablecloth over the side, where all my old comrades could see me; later I thought I would rather be the deckhand who stood on the end of the stage plank with the coil of rope in his hand, because he was particularly conspicuous. But these were only daydreams—they were too heavenly to be contemplated as real possibilities. By and by one of our boys went away. He was not heard of for a long time. At last he turned up as apprentice engineer or striker on a steamboat. This thing shook the bottom out of all my Sunday-school teachings. That boy had been notoriously worldly, and I just the reverse; yet he was exalted to this eminence, and I left in obscurity and misery. There was nothing generous about this fellow in his greatness. He would always manage to have a rusty bolt to scrub while his boat tarried at our town, and he would sit on the inside guard and scrub it, where we could all see him and envy him and loathe him. And whenever his boat was laid up he would come home and swell around the town in his blackest and greasiest clothes, so that nobody could help remembering that he was a steamboatman; and he used all sorts of steamboat technicalities in his talk, as if he were so used to them that he forgot common people could not understand them. He would speak of the labboard side of a horse in an easy, natural way that would make one wish he was dead. And he was always talking about "St. Looey" like an old citizen; he would refer casually to occasions when he "was coming down Fourth Street," or when he was "passing by the Planter's House," or when there was a fire and he took a turn on the brakes of old "The Big Missouri"; and then he would go on and lie about how many towns the size of ours were burned down there that day. Two or three of the boys had long been persons of consideration among us because they had been to St. Louis once and had a vague general knowledge of its wonders, but the day of their glory was over now. They lapsed into a humble silence, and learned to disappear when the ruthless cub engineer approached. This fellow had money, too, and hair oil. Also an ignorant silver watch and a showy brass watch chain. He wore a leather belt and used no suspenders. If ever a youth was cordially admired and hated by his comrades, this one was. No girl could withstand his charms. He cut out every boy in the village. When his boat blew up at last, it diffused tranquil contentment among us such as we had not known for months. But when he came home the next week, alive, renowned and appeared in church all battered up and bandaged, a shining hero, stared at and wondered over by everybody, it seemed to us that the partiality of Providence for an undeserving reptile had reached a point where it was open to criticism.

This creature's career could produce but one result, and it speedily followed. Boy after boy managed to get on the river. The minister's son became an engineer. The doctor's and the postmaster's sons became mud clerks; the wholesale liquor dealer's son became a barkeeper on a boat; four sons of the chief merchant, and two sons of the county judge, became pilots. Pilot was the grandest position of all. The pilot, even in those days of trivial wages, had a princely salary—from a hundred and fifty to two hundred and fifty dollars a month, and no board to pay. Two months of his wages would pay a preacher's salary for a year. Now some of us were left disconsolate. We could not get on the river—at least our parents would not let us.

So by and by I ran away. I said I never would come home again till I was a pilot and could come in glory. But somehow I could not manage it. I went meekly aboard a few of the boats that lay packed together like sardines at the long St. Louis wharf, and very humbly inquired for the pilots, but got only a cold shoulder and short words from mates and clerks. I had to make the best of this sort of treatment for the time being, but I had comforting daydreams of a future, when I should be a great and honored pilot, with plenty of money, and could kill some of these mates and clerks and pay for them.

---

1. When Twain was a boy, what was the "permanent ambition" among his comrades?

2. What ambitions were transient?

3. As other ambitions faded out, which ambitions remained?

4. How does Twain describe the "magnificent Mississippi"?

5. How does the town react to the steamboat's arrival?

6. When the boy returned as an apprentice engineer, how was he received? Why did the other boys respond to him the way they did?

7. What reason did Twain give for running away?

8. Why do you suppose that this piece is called "A Boy's Ambition"? What made it typical for a boy in that time? Could a girl have aspired to this ambition in the 1800's? What about today?

9. In Mark Twain's era, running away to join the circus or becoming a steamboat worker were considered fantasy careers. What are the fantasy careers for today's teens? Is there a difference based on gender?

Mark Twain 1835–1910

Mark Twain is the pen name for Samuel Langhorne Clemens, one of America's best known writers. He grew up in Hannibal, Missouri. Twain worked as a riverboat pilot, a printer, prospected for gold, and gave lectures around the world. His pen name came from the cry of Mississippi riverboatmen: "By the mark, twain!" — assessing the river as two fathoms deep. His two most famous novels are *The Adventures of Tom Sawyer* and *The Adventures of Huckleberry Finn*. His work is considered to be classic American literature.

Journal entry:
    Mark Twain gave this advice about careers:
      "Make your vocation your vacation."
    Explain what you think he meant.

Lego

from *The New Yorker Magazine*

January 14, 1991

Growing up in Queens in the sixties and seventies, Francie Berger knew exactly what she wanted from life: more Lego building bricks. She received her first set, a gift from her parents, when she was three. Gradually, she added to her holdings. She liked to build houses, and she wished that she could build bigger ones. As a teen-ager, she began writing to Lego Systems, Inc., the American division of the toy's Danish manufacturer, to ask if she could order, say, two million standard red bricks. The company said that she could not. In college—where she majored in architecture, figuring that building real houses was the adult occupation that came closest to her favorite activity—she wrote more letters. At some point, it occurred to her that she might be able to get a job at Lego itself. She began calling the company on a monthly basis, and she once dropped by its headquarters, in Enfield, Connecticut. "By then," Berger recalls, "they knew who I was." The person who was dispatched to get rid of her told her to send a résumé, by mail, after graduation. Undeterred, she spent part of her senior year using Lego bricks to build a scale model of a farm. The model served both as her senior thesis and as a job application. Seeing no way out, Lego hired her, in 1984, for a three-week trial period. She has been with the company ever since, and is perhaps the most satisfied worker in the history of employment.

Berger's job is building things out of Lego bricks. Her works include the six-foot-tall red-bearded pirate that stands in the Lego department of F. A. O. Schwartz, on Fifth Avenue, and the six-foot-tall roller coaster, part of an animal amusement park, in the window of the Toys "R" Us in Herald Square. They also include the thirteen-foot-tall (and twenty-seven-and-a-half-foot-wide) replica of the United States Capitol which, along with a number of models of other national landmarks and monuments, recently spent a little more than a month on display at A. & S. Plaza, on West Thirty-third Street. All these models are made entirely of Lego bricks (the Capitol contains more than half a million), and all were assembled by Lego's staff of model-designers and model-builders, of which Berger is the head. The company uses the models as promotions. The Capitol was part of a travelling show that visited ten shopping malls during 1990 and is now in the process of being split up and parcelled out to various children's museums. Most people, upon seeing the Capitol model, have two reactions. The first is "Hey, the White House!" The second is "I can't believe somebody built that out of Lego bricks!"

"When we build a model, we don't use any bricks that you can't buy in stores, and we don't alter them or cut them or do anything weird to them," Berger told us not long ago, when we went to visit her in Enfield. "First, the designers draw the model on special graph paper that is scaled to the bricks. Then they build a prototype without gluing it, to prove that it can be done. Then the model-builders make an exact copy and glue it together. They also make sure it's as hollow as possible, so it will be easier to move around." Some of the moving around is done in two custom-built air-ride semitrailers.

Lego's model-builders work at long tables that can be raised and lowered hydraulically. The tables are connected to an elaborate ventilation system that whisks away fumes from the glue, which is kept in Elmer's bottles but is actually methyl ethyl ketone, a potent solvent that causes the plastic of the bricks to fuse. Once a model has been glued, it can be taken out into the parking lot of a shopping mall, say, and washed down with a garden hose or scrubbed with Formula 409. It can also be left outside for just about as long as you like. The visitors' parking lot at the company headquarters is furnished with an earlier version of the Capitol model, which is kept there year-round.

Francie Berger is thirty years old. She wears aviator glasses and, occasionally, white go-go boots. Her hair is brown and is cut in a long shag. In her office she has a desk, a telephone, a lamp, a photograph of herself chatting with the architect Philip Johnson, some other things, and dozens of bins containing Lego bricks, all sorted by color and type. The Lego building system consists at the moment of roughly thirteen hundred different elements, and Berger is allowed to have as many of any of them as she wants. If she uses up all the pieces in one of her bins, she simply walks into another part of the building and gets more.

Berger's life thus far has been fashioned almost entirely of Lego bricks. When she was married, in 1988, her wedding invitation was decorated with a photograph of a three-foot-tall red Lego hippopotamus bride and groom. Building the hippopotamuses took Berger and her fiance, a welder, more than two months. On top of the couple's wedding cake was a smaller Lego model, of a human bride and groom. When other Lego employees get married, they often borrow this decoration for their cakes. Each December, Berger and her husband use Lego bricks to build a seasonal tableau beneath their Christmas tree.

Berger does most of her work in her office, but sometimes she travels to shopping malls or state fairs and builds models while people watch. She and a colleague recently built a copy of the Connecticut Capitol at a fair not far from the company's headquarters. The model was eight and a half feet high, ten feet wide, and six feet deep. Building it consumed a hundred and ninety-two person-hours of labor over twelve days. While Berger and her colleague worked, people gathered around to watch and ask questions. Many of the people wanted to know what they would have to do to get a job at Lego. Every year, Berger receives dozens of letters from children, art students, engineers, architects, and others, all wanting to know the same thing. "A lot of kids ask what kind of college courses they should take," Berger told us. "When I write back, I just kind of explain how I got my job. It was a little unorthodox, but it worked for me."

Berger's job didn't exist when she was hired. At that time, all the models used by Lego's American division were made in Denmark and shipped to the United States. To Berger, that seemed nutty. Why not build those models right here in America, and why not let Francie Berger build them? Today, she supervises two other designers and half a dozen full-time model-builders. All these people are, in effect, manifestations of her determination to spend her life doing the thing she likes best.

---

1. When did Francie Berger know "exactly what she wanted from life"?

2. When did Francie first begin writing to Lego? What did she ask them for?

3. What was Francie's major in college?

4. Explain, step by step, how Francie pursued her idea of getting a job at Lego. Why do you suppose that persistence paid off in her case?

5. How did Francie spend part of her senior year in college? What purpose did this project fulfill?

6. Why is she, "perhaps the most satisfied worker in the history of employment"?

7. List several of the large models that Francie and her staff have completed. Have you ever seen any of these models? If so, explain where it was and what it looked like.

8. What process do the model builders follow when executing a project?

9. What impresses you about this woman who was determined to spend her life "doing the thing she likes best"?

10. Joseph Campbell advises people to "follow their bliss" when pursuing a career. He wrote: "I always tell my students to follow their bliss, where the deep sense of being is from, and where your body and soul want to go." Francie Berger certainly followed this advice. What lesson could we learn from her story?

11. Remember Francie's story as you are considering careers to investigate in Chapter Six. Pay attention to your passions and values as listed on page 147 of *Career Choices*. If surfing, skateboarding or skiing are one of your passions, it might be difficult to incorporate that into your work. For example, how many professional surfers are there? Analyze the elements of your favorite activity or passion and see if you can incorporate some of those into your work. For example someone who is passionate about surfing might pursue a career that incorporates some of the following:

   the outdoors

   the ocean

   taking risks

   solitude

   physical involvement

   challenge

patience

What are some of the elements of your passions?

Writing Assignment

The story of how Francie obtained her job is one of a dream come true. Most people would read this and think that it could never happen to them. Review your bull's eye chart on page 27 of **Career Choices**. Now, let your imagination run wild; write a description of a job, whether you think it exists or not, that would meet your fantasy. What would you do? How would you spend an average day at this job?

Journal entry:
> Think about the men and women at work right now in America. There are people on the job at all times of the day and night, performing thousands of different tasks. What kinds of jobs come to mind when you think about work? Shut your eyes for a minute and think about it. What do you see? Describe that vision.

I Hear America Singing

by Walt Whitman

I hear America singing, the varied carols I hear,
Those of mechanics, each one singing his as it should be blithe and strong,
The carpenter singing his as he measures his plank or beam,
The mason singing his as he makes ready for work, or leaves off work,
The boatman singing what belongs to him in his boat, the deckhand singing on the steamboat deck,
The shoemaker singing as he sits on his bench, the hatter singing as he stands,
The wood-cutter's song, the ploughboy's on his way in the morning, or at noon intermission or at sundown,
The delicious singing of the mother, or of the young wife at work, or of the girl sewing or washing,
Each singing what belongs to him or her and to none else,
The day what belongs to the day—at night the party of young fellows, robust, friendly,
Singing with open mouths their strong melodious songs.

1. This poem evokes many images of people across the nation at work. Does it seem like the people enjoy their work? How does Whitman show that?

2. How would you describe the mood of this poem? Is it happy, sad, serious, or lighthearted? What words does Whitman use to show us the mood of these people?

3. Walt Whitman lived from 1819 to 1892. How was a worker's life different at that time? We have moved from an industrial age to one of technology, and as a result, some of these careers no longer exist. Re-read the poem, and identify the careers that you don't think are viable options in today's world.

4. In your journal entry, did you think of both men and women working? What can you tell about the working roles of men and women in the era Whitman lived?

Copy Change

Review the careers that you have researched or read about in Chapter Six of *Career Choices*. Re-write the poem changing some of the careers mentioned to more common ones in America today. Be sure to make it more inclusive and non-sexist, as well.

Art Activity

Choose one medium (pencil, pastels, charcoal, construction paper, crayons) to depict a scene from the poem on the left-hand side of your paper and a scene from your poem on the right-hand side. You can focus on one image in particular, or make a collage of several images.

Walt Whitman 1819–1892

Walt Whitman was born on Long Island and raised in Brooklyn, New York. When he was twenty-seven he became the editor of a newspaper but was discharged because of his strong opposition to slavery. After relocating to New Orleans to accept a position on a newspaper there, he traveled across America to observe the diverse landscapes and peoples. In 1850 he started writing poetry full-time and left journalism. When *Leaves of Grass* was published in 1855, it was met with mixed reactions. Emerson was enthusiastic about it and said, "the most extraordinary piece of wit and wisdom that America has yet contributed." But others were offended by Whitman's lack of rhyme and meter. Whitman was an important part of the Transcendentalist movement. He wrote, "The proof of a poet is that his country absorbs him as affectionately as he absorbed it." After his death, his work in *Leaves of Grass* came to be regarded as one of the best collections of poetry ever written.

Journal Entry:
> Have you ever been offered something that seemed too good to be true? What was it? Did you accept the offer hastily or did you evaluate the options, pros and cons, and the probability of success? If you accepted in haste, did you regret it later? Describe your situation.

The Monkey's Paw

By W. W. JACOBS

A Play Based on the Story

Characters:

MR. WHITE, ... an elderly man
MRS. WHITE, ... his wife
HERBERT, ... their 21-year-old son
SERGEANT MORRIS, ... a retired military officer
MR. PARSONS, ... a 35-year-old man

SCENE ONE

It is a rainy, windy evening in a rural part of England. Inside a cozy house, a fire burns brightly in the living-room fireplace. Mr. White and Herbert, his 21-year-old-son, are playing chess. Mrs. White is knitting. The dining table is set for four people.

MR. WHITE: Listen to the wind. Perhaps Morris won't come over tonight, after all. This place is so far out of the way, and the rain has turned the roads to mud.

HERBERT: Who is Morris?

MRS. WHITE: Your father knew him years ago when they went to school together. For the past 30 years or so, Sergeant Morris has been living in India. Now he's retired and living in

England again. Your father ran into him in London last week.

(There is a knock on the door.)

HERBERT: There he is!

(Mr. White gets up, goes to the door, and lets in Sergeant Morris. There is a haunted look in Morris' eyes.)

MR. WHITE: Morris, old boy, it's good to see you. Come in, and let me hang up your coat.

MORRIS: Thank you. *(He takes off his coat.)* It's nasty weather out there.

(Mr. White hangs up Morris' coat Then he leads his old friend over to his wife.)

MR. WHITE: This is Martha, my wife.

MRS. WHITE: Welcome to our home.

MORRIS: It's a pleasure to be here, and a pleasure to meet you at last.

MR. WHITE: And this is Herbert, our son.

HERBERT: How do you do, sir?

MORRIS: Why, you look like your father when he was a lad of 20 years old.

MR. WHITE: Sit down by the fire, and I'll get you some whiskey.

(Morris sits by the fire near Mrs. White. Herbert sits across from them. Mr. White pours a glass of whiskey and hands it to Morris. Then he sits beside Herbert.)

MR. WHITE *(to his wife):* When Morris left for India, he was an innocent young man, eager for adventure. Now look at him. I'll bet he's seen a thing or two.

MRS. WHITE *(politely):* He doesn't seem to have come to any harm.

MR. WHITE: I'd like to go to India myself, just to look around a bit.

(Morris drinks his whiskey quickly.)

MORRIS: It's better where you are.

MR. WHITE *(refilling Morris' empty glass):* But it sounds so interesting and . . . well, strange, over there. What was it you began to tell me the other day about a monkey's paw? That certainly sounded mysterious.

MRS. WHITE *(curiously)*: A monkey's paw?

MORRIS: I don't think you want to hear about it. It's just a bit of Far Eastern magic.

HERBERT *(amused)*: Magic? Do you really believe in magic?

MORRIS *(taking something from his pocket)*: To look at it, it's just an ordinary little paw. *(He holds up the dried-up paw of a monkey.)*

HERBERT *(taking the paw)*: It looks ordinary enough to me.

MR. WHITE *(taking the paw from his son)*: What is special about it? *(He looks it over and puts it on the table beside him.)*

MORRIS: An old holy man put a spell on it. He believed that fate rules our lives. He wanted to prove that anyone who tries to interfere with fate will be sorry. He put a spell on that paw so that three different people could each have three wishes granted by it.

HERBERT *(laughing)*: Well, why don't you make three wishes, sir?

MORRIS *(turning pale)*: I already have.

MRS. WHITE: Were your three wishes granted?

MORRIS *(after drinking more whiskey)*: Yes.

MRS. WHITE: Has anybody else wished on it?

MORRIS: Yes. One man got his three wishes. I don't know what the first two wishes were. But the third one was for death. That is how I got the paw.

(The others are silent for a few moments.)

MR. WHITE *(finally)*: If you've had your three wishes, Morris, it's no good to you any longer. Why do you keep it?

MORRIS: I once thought of selling it, but I don't think I will. It has caused enough harm already.

MRS. WHITE: If you could have three more wishes, would you take them?

MORRIS: No, I would not!

(Morris suddenly goes to the table beside Mr. White, picks up

the paw, and throws it upon the fire. Mr. White quickly grabs the paw out of the fire.)

MR. WHITE: Why did you do that?

MORRIS: It's better to let it burn than to let it ruin lives.

MR. WHITE: If you don't want it, give it to me.

MORRIS: Believe me. I threw it into the fire for good reason. If you keep it, don't blame me for what happens.

MR. WHITE *(looking closely at the paw)*: How do you make a wish on it?

MORRIS: You simply hold the paw in your right hand and wish aloud.

MRS. WHITE *(standing up)*: Excuse me while I put dinner on the table. *(She smiles at her husband.)* Why don't you wish for four pairs of hands for me?

(Mr. White and Herbert laugh. Sergeant Morris, however, looks alarmed.)

MORRIS *(taking Mr. White by the arm)*: Don't laugh. If you must wish, at least wish for something sensible.

SCENE TWO

It is later that evening. Sergeant Morris has just left the house. Mrs. White is wiping one last crumb off the dining table. Mr. White walks over to the fire and lights his pipe. Herbert walks over to the piano and sits on the piano bench.

HERBERT: Sergeant Morris certainly had some strange tales to tell. I'm afraid, Father, that the tale about the monkey's paw is no more truthful than the others.

MRS. WHITE *(to her husband)*: Did you give him anything for it?

MR. WHITE: *(embarrassed)*: Just a small amount of money. He said he didn't want it, but I made him take it. He kept urging me to throw the thing away.

HERBERT: A magic monkey's paw! That's a laugh! Why don't you wish to be an emperor, Father. Then Mother couldn't boss you around.

MRS. WHITE: You watch your manners, young man.

MR. WHITE *(taking the monkey's paw from his pocket):* I don't know what to wish for, and that's a fact. It seems to me I've got everything I want.

HERBERT: Wouldn't you be glad if the mortgage on this house were paid for?

MR. WHITE: Well, yes, but—

HERBERT: Then wish for nine thousand pounds.

(Herbert winks at his mother. Then he plays three dramatic chords on the piano. His father looks a bit embarrassed.)

MR. WHITE *(holding up the paw):* I wish for nine thousand pounds. *(He quickly drops the paw, with a cry.)* No!

MRS. WHITE *(going over to him):* What is the matter?

MR. WHITE: It moved! *(He looks with disgust at the paw on the floor.)* As I made the wish, it twisted in my hand like a snake!

HERBERT*(Picking up the paw):* Well. I don't see the money. (He *puts the paw on the mantel over the fireplace.)* I'm going to bed now. I've got a busy day at work tomorrow. *(He goes upstairs.)*

MRS. WHITE *(to her husband):* Are you feeling all right?

MR. WHITE: I've just had a bit of a shock, that's all. I'll probably feel fine after a good night's sleep.

(The wind blows outside. A shutter bangs against the house.)

SCENE THREE

The next morning, it is sunny, and warm. Mr. and Mrs. White and Herbert are eating breakfast. Mr. White looks as if he didn't get much sleep. Mrs. White is trying to cheer him up.

MRS. WHITE: I suppose all old soldiers like to tell tall tales. I can't believe we listened to such nonsense last night. How could a dead animal's paw grant wishes? And even if it could, how could nine thousand pounds possibly hurt us?

HERBERT *(joking):* It might fall from the sky, on Father's head.

MR. WHITE *(not smiling):* That's not how it happens. The wishes come about so naturally, that they seem to be coincidences.

HERBERT *(getting up from the table):* Well, I'm off to work now. Don't spend the nine thousand pounds before I get back. *(His mother laughs.)* I'll see you this evening. *(He goes out the front door.)*

MRS. WHITE *(to her husband):* I suppose Herbert will still be making funny remarks about the monkey's paw when he comes home.

MR. WHITE: Maybe so. Still, the thing moved in my hand.

MRS. WHITE *(gently):* You *thought* it did.

MR. WHITE: It did! I swear it did!

SCENE FOUR

That evening, the dining table is set for three people. Mrs. White is looking out the front window. She suddenly looks startled.

MR. WHITE: What is the matter, dear?

MRS. WHITE: There's a man standing near our front gate. He seems to be wondering whether or not to enter.

MR. WHITE: I'll go out and ask him what he wants.

MRS. WHITE *(smiling):* Maybe he is bringing us the nine thousand pounds.

(Mr White opens the front door and calls to the man outside.)

MR. WHITE: Hello, there! May I help you?

(Mr Parsons appears at the door. He is about 35 years old.)

PARSONS *(nervously):* Mr. White?

MR. WHITE: Yes?

PARSONS: My name is Edward Parsons. I was asked to call on you.

MR. WHITE: Come in.

(Mr. Parsons enters and nods at Mrs. White.)

PARSONS: I'm from Maw and Meggins.

MRS. WHITE *(alarmed):* Why, that's where Herbert works! is anything the matter? Has anything happened to Herbert?

MR. WHITE: Now, calm down, my dear. *(He turns to Parsons.)* You haven't brought bad news, have you?

PARSONS: I'm sorry. There's been an accident.

MR. WHITE: Is he hurt?

PARSONS *(quietly):* He is badly hurt, but he is not in any pain.

MRS. WHITE: Thank goodness for that! Thank . . . . *(She stops.)* Oh, no! You don't mean . . . . *(She sits on the sofa.)*

MR. WHITE *(to Parsons):* What happened?

PARSONS: He was caught in the machinery. He was killed instantly.

(Mr White sits beside his wife and holds her hands. They are both too shocked to speak at first. After a silence, Mr. White turns to Mr. Parsons.)

MR. WHITE: He was our only child.

PARSONS *(uneasily):* I am so sorry. The company wanted me to express their deepest sympathy.

MR. WHITE *(in a daze):* Yes. Thank you.

PARSONS: Maw and Meggins were not responsible for the accident. But they appreciate the work your son has done for them. They wish to give you a sum of money. Of course it won't make up for your great loss, but—

(Mr. White gets to his feet it with a look of horror.)

MR. WHITE: How much is the sum of money?

PARSONS: Nine thousand pounds.

(Mrs. White screams. Mr. White stands still for a moment. Then he falls to the floor in a faint.)

SCENE FIVE

Two weeks later, in the middle of the night, Mrs. White enters the living room. She is wearing a bathrobe, and she is crying. A few moments later, Mr. White appears.

MR. WHITE *(gently):* Come back to bed, dear. It is cold down here.

MRS. WHITE: It is colder for our son in the cemetery.

MR. WHITE: Martha, you are worrying yourself sick over Herbert. He is gone. We must face it. Worrying won't bring him back.

(Mrs. White suddenly stops crying. She turns to her husband

with a wild look in her eyes.)

MRS. WHITE: The monkey's paw! Where is it?

MR. WHITE *(surprised)*: I'm not sure. *(Pause.)* I think I left it on the mantel over the fireplace. Why?

MRS. WHITE *(to herself)*: Why didn't I think of it before?

MR. WHITE: Think of what?

MRS. WHITE: The other two wishes. You have had only one wish!

MR. WHITE *(shocked)*: Wasn't that one enough?

MRS. WHITE: No! *(She finds the monkey's paw on the mantel and holds it out to her husband.)* Wish for Herbert to be alive again!

MR. WHITE: Are you crazy!

MRS. WHITE: Your first wish came true. Why shouldn't your second wish come true?

MR. WHITE *(uneasy)*: It was . . . it was just a coincidence.

MRS. WHITE *(fiercely)*: Wish!

MR. WHITE: It is foolish and wicked.

MRS. WHITE *(putting the paw in his hand)*: Wish!

MR. WHITE *(holding up the paw)*: I wish my son alive. *(He drops the paw.)* It moved again!

SCENE SIX

An hour later, Mr. and Mrs. White are still in the living room. Mrs. White is looking out the window. Mr. White is sitting by the fireplace, although the fire has gone out.

MRS. WHITE *(turning to her husband)*: How long have we been waiting?

MR. WHITE: Over an hour. *(He goes over to her.)* It's no use, dear. Please go back to bed. Don't torture yourself by hoping for the impossible.

(Mrs. White nods sadly. As they both start upstairs, there is a scratching sound at the front door. Mrs. White stops and turns.)

MRS. WHITE: What's that?

MR. WHITE *(uneasy)*: It must be a rat trying to get in.

(There is a knock on the door.)

MRS. WHITE: It's Herbert!

(Mrs. White tries to run to the door, but her husband holds her back.

MR. WHITE: What are you trying to do?

MRS. WHITE: It's our son! I forgot that the cemetery is two miles away. That is why it has taken him so long to get here. Let me go!

MR. WHITE *(holding her back):* You didn't see Herbert after the accident. I did. I couldn't recognize him, except by his clothing. And now he's been dead for two weeks. Don't let him in! He won't be the same!

MRS. WHITE: Are you afraid of your own son?

(There are three loud knocks on the door. Mrs. White breaks free and runs to the door. She tries to slide back the bolt, but it is too high for her to reach.)

MRS. WHITE *(calling to her husband):* Help me!

(Mr. White quickly begins searching for the monkey's paw, which he dropped in front of the fireplace. Meanwhile, Mrs. White moves a chair to the door and stands on it. As she slides back the bolt, Mr. White finds the paw and holds it up.)

MR. WHITE: I wish my son dead—and back in his grave!

(Mr. White gets down off the chair and pulls it to one side. She opens the door, and a cold wind rushes into the house.)

MRS. WHITE *(mournfully):* Herbert? Where are you? Herbert?

(Mr. White goes to her side. Then he goes out the front door. In a few moments he is back inside.)

MR. WHITE: There is no one here, my dear. And the road beyond the front gate is empty.

THE END

1. How does the opening set the mood for the story?
2. Herbert is amused by the idea that the monkey's paw has magic powers. Why is this ironic?
3. What three wishes did Mr. White make? Were the wishes wise choices?
4. What thoughts must have been running through Mr. White's mind as the knocking continued at the door? He had to make a quick decision. What choices did he have? Would you have made the same choice considering the circumstances? Why or why not? Review a copy of the decision making chart on page 173 of *Career Choices* and complete a chart for the problem: What should the White's do about the knocking at the door?

Writing Dialogue

Did Mr. White gather enough information before making the decision to use the monkey's paw? If you were Mr. White, what other data would you need before making your first wish? What might Morris have told him, had he been asked? Write a dialogue between Morris and Mr. White which completes the following line of questioning:

MR. WHITE: Tell me Morris, old chap, what were your three wishes? Come to think of it, what were the first two wishes of the first bloke who had that paw?
MORRIS:

When finished, pair up with a classmate and read your scripts to the class until all dialogues have been read. How many people had their characters continue and make the three wishes? How many decided to throw the paw into the fire?

Writing Assignment

Choose one of the following topics to discuss in a five paragraph essay. Before beginning, read the guidelines for writing a five paragraph essay.

A. Do you believe in fate? Or do you believe we can make our life what we want if we make wise choices? Explain your belief in a fully developed essay.

B. Discuss the meaning of the following in an essay: Saint Theresa said that there are more tears shed over answered prayers than unanswered ones. What did she mean? Do you agree or disagree?

The Five Paragraph Essay: the basic structure

Paragraph 1: paragraph of introduction

> A. Hook: a way to get the reader's attention, it can be a:
>
> quotation
>
> anecdote that is fictional but appropriate
>
> a statistic
>
> a question
>
> B. The thesis is the focus of the entire essay. This includes one or two sentences that address the issue and breaks the topic into three sub-parts.

Paragraph 2, 3, 4: the paragraphs of the body

> Each body paragraph is about one of the three sub-parts.
>
> Paragraph 2 is about the first sub-topic in the thesis.
>
> Paragraph 3 is about the second sub-topic.
>
> Paragraph 4 is about the third sub-topic.

Paragraph 5: the conclusion

A. Include a brief summary of the three sub-parts. Try to say this in a new way, use synonyms.

B. While conclusions should not go far beyond what you have explained or proven in the body of your essay, they should take the reader a little beyond what has been covered. They can contain:

> an evaluation
>
> a prediction
>
> a warning

W.W. Jacobs 1863–1943

W. W. Jacobs was born in London, England. As a child, he lived in a house on a Thames River dock where he heard tales of foreign lands told by seafarers passing through. As an adult, Jacobs made use of this experience by writing strange tales of his own. Many of his stories combine everyday life with elements of the supernatural. "The Monkey's Paw" is one such tale. It was first published in 1902 and made into a play one year later.

Journal entry:
Throughout life we have to make choices about which path to follow. What are some of the most important decisions you will make:

next year
in ten years

Think of a choice that you made in the last year and write about it, the options you had and the process of thought you used for making that choice.

The Road Not Taken

by Robert Frost

Two roads diverged in a yellow wood,
And sorry I could not travel both
And be one traveler, long I stood
And looked down one as far as I could
To where it bent in the undergrowth;

Then took the other, as just as fair,
And having perhaps the better claim,
Because it was grassy and wanted wear;
Though as for that, the passing there
Had worn them really about the same,

Continued

And both that morning equally lay
In leaves no step had trodden black.
Oh, I kept the first for another day!
Yet knowing how way leads on to way,
I doubted if I should ever come back.

I shall be telling this with a sigh
Somewhere ages and ages hence:
Two roads diverged in a wood, and I—
I took the one less traveled by,
And that has made all the difference.

---

1. What is the physical landscape described in this poem?

2. How are the two paths described?

3. Are the two paths easily distinguished, one from the other?

4. Describe the path the author took. Why did he choose that path?

5. If the landscape is symbolic, how could you interpret this poem?

6. What does "with a sigh" indicate?

7. Describe a choice similar to Frost's that you have had to make. (His choice involved two alternatives.) After explaining which choice you made, discuss the consequences of that decision. Did you gather data, list all of the options, evaluate the options and probable outcomes before finalizing your decision? In retrospect, are you happy with the choice that you made?

Robert Frost 1874–1963

Robert Frost, though strongly associated with the idiom and landscape of New England, was born in California. Frost lived mostly in New Hampshire and Vermont but also spent significant periods of time in Michigan and Florida. He was named for Robert E. Lee, the great confederate general. Frost was raised a New Englander and the titles of many of his books insist on the identification, *North of Boston, New Hampshire,* and *A Boy's Will* (the phrase comes from a poem by Longfellow who was born in Maine). Frost was unique in his power to combine a modernist sensibility and learning with a knack for the truly popular. In "Mending Wall" he became the only modern poet who could genuinely be said to have written a proverb: "Good fences make good neighbors." He is considered one of the best American poets of the 20th century.

Journal entry:
>   Have you ever made a choice or heard of someone (on
>   the news perhaps) who made a choice that turned out
>   to have life threatening consequences?
>
>   What was that choice? What happened or nearly hap-
>   pened? Was all the information available at the time
>   evaluated before the choice was made?

To Build a Fire

by Jack London

Day had broken cold and gray, exceedingly cold and gray, when the man turned aside from the main Yukon trail and climbed the high earth-bank, where a dim and little-travelled trail led eastward through the fat spruce timberland. It was a steep bank, and he paused for breath at the top, excusing the act to himself by looking at his watch. It was nine o'clock. There was no sun nor hint of sun, though there was not a cloud in the sky. It was a clear day, and yet there seemed an intangible pall over the face of things, a subtle gloom that made the day dark, and that was due to the absence of sun. This fact did not worry the man. He was used to the lack of sun. It had been days since he had seen the sun, and he knew that a few more days must pass before that cheerful orb, due south, would just peep above the sky line and dip immediately from view.

The man flung a look back along the way he had come. The Yukon lay a mile wide and hidden under three feet of ice. On top of this ice were as many feet of snow. It was all pure white, rolling in gentle undulations where the ice jams of the freeze-up had formed. North and south, as far as his eye could see, it was unbroken white, save for a dark hairline that curved and twisted from around the spruce-covered island to the south, and that curved and twisted away into the north, where it disappeared behind another spruce-covered island. This dark hairline was the trail—the main trail—that led south five hundred miles to the Chilcoot Pass, Dyea, and salt water; and that led north seventy miles to Dawson, and still on to the north a thousand miles to Nulato, and finally to St. Michael, on Bering Sea, a thousand miles and half a thousand more.

But all this—the mysterious, far-reaching hairline trail, the absence of sun from the sky, the tremendous cold, and the strangeness and weirdness of it all—made no impression on the man. It was not because he was long used to it. He was a newcomer in the land, a *chechaquo*, and this was his first winter. The trouble with him was that he was without imagination. He was quick and alert in the things of life, but only in the things, and not in the significances. Fifty degrees below zero meant eighty-odd degrees of frost. Such fact impressed him as being cold and uncomfortable, and that was all. It did not lead him to meditate upon his frailty as a creature of temperature, and upon man's frailty in general, able only to live within certain narrow limits of heat and cold; and from there on it did not lead him to the conjectural field of immortality and man's place in the universe. Fifty degrees below zero stood for a bite of frost that hurt and that must be guarded against by the use of mittens, ear flaps, warm moccasins, and thick socks. Fifty degrees below zero was to him just precisely fifty degrees below zero. That there should be anything more to it than that was a thought that never entered his head.

As he turned to go, he spat speculatively. There was a sharp, explosive crackle that startled him. He spat again. And again, in the air, before it could fall to the snow, the spittle crackled. He knew that at fifty below spittle cracked on the snow, but this spittle had crackled in the air. Undoubtedly it was colder than fifty below—how much colder he did not know.

But the temperature did not matter. He was bound for the old claim on the left fork of Henderson Creek, where the boys were already. They had come over across the divide from the Indian Creek country, while he had come the roundabout way to take a look at the possibilities of getting out logs in the spring from the islands in the Yukon. He would be in to camp by six o'clock; a bit after dark, it was true, but the boys would be there, a fire would be going, and a hot supper would be ready. As for lunch, he pressed his hand against the protruding bundle under his jacket. It was also under his shirt, wrapped up in a handkerchief and lying against the naked skin. It was the only way to keep the biscuits from freezing. He smiled agreeably to himself as he thought of those biscuits, each cut open and sopped in bacon grease, and each enclosing a generous slice of red bacon.

He plunged in among the big spruce trees. The trail was faint. A foot of snow had fallen since the last sled had passed over, and he was glad he was without a sled, travelling light. In fact, he carried nothing but the lunch wrapped in the hand-kerchief. He was surprised, however, at the cold. It certainly was cold, he concluded, as he rubbed his numb nose and cheekbones with his mittened hand. He was a warm-whiskered man, but the hair on his face did not protect the high cheek-bones and the eager nose that thrust itself aggressively into the frosty air.

At the man's heels trotted a dog, a big native husky, the proper wolf dog, gray-coated and without any visible or temperamental difference from its brother, the wild wolf. The animal was depressed by the tremendous cold. It knew that it was no time for travelling. Its instinct told it a truer tale than was told to the man by the man's judgment. In reality, it was not merely colder than fifty below zero; it was colder than sixty below, than seventy below. It was seventy-five below zero. Since the freezing point is thirty-two above zero, it meant that one hundred and seven degrees of frost obtained. The dog did not know anything about thermometers. Possibly in its brain there was no sharp consciousness of a condition of very cold such as was in the man's brain. But the brute had its instinct. It experienced a vague but menacing apprehension that subdued it and made it slink along at the man's heels, and that made it question eagerly every unwonted movement of the man as if expecting him to go into camp or to seek shelter somewhere and build a fire. The dog had learned fire, and it wanted fire, or else to burrow under the snow and cuddle its warmth away from the air.

The frozen moisture of its breathing had settled on its fur in a fine powder of frost, and especially were its jowls, muzzle, and eyelashes whitened by its crystalled breath. The man's red beard and mustache were likewise frosted, but more solidly, the deposit taking the form of ice and increasing with every warm, moist breath he exhaled. Also, the man was chewing tobacco, and the muzzle of ice held his lips so rigidly that he was unable to clear his chin when he expelled the juice. The result was that a crystal beard of the color and solidity of amber was increasing its length on his chin. If he fell down it would shatter itself, like glass, into brittle fragments. But he did not mind the appendage. It was the penalty all tobacco chewers paid in that country, and he had been out before in two cold snaps. They had not been so cold as this, he knew, but by the spirit thermometer at Sixty Mile he knew they had been registered at fifty below and at fifty-five.

He held on through the level stretch of woods for several miles, crossed a wide flat of nigger heads, and dropped down a bank to the frozen bed of a small stream. This was Henderson Creek, and he knew he was ten miles from the forks. He looked at his watch. It was ten o'clock. He was making four miles an hour, and he calculated that he would arrive at the forks at half-past twelve. He decided to celebrate that event by eating his lunch there.

The dog dropped in again at his heels, with a trail drooping discouragement, as the man swung along the creek bed. The furrow of the old sled trail was plainly visible, but a dozen inches of snow covered the marks of the last runners. In a month no man had come up or down that silent creek. The man held steadily on. He was not much given to thinking, and just then particularly he had nothing to think about save that he would eat lunch at the forks and that at six o'clock he would be in camp with the boys. There was nobody to talk to; and, had there been, speech would have been impossible because of the ice muzzle on his mouth. So he continued monotonously to chew tobacco and to increase the length of his amber beard.

Once in a while the thought reiterated itself that it was very cold and that he had never experienced such cold. As he walked along he rubbed his cheekbones and nose with the back of his mittened hand. He did this automatically, now and again changing hands. But, rub as he would, the instant he stopped his cheekbones went numb, and the following instant the end of his nose went numb. He was sure to frost his cheeks; he knew that, and experienced a pang of regret that he had not devised a nose strap of the sort Bud wore in cold snaps. Such a strap passed across the cheeks, as well, and saved them. But it didn't matter much, after all. What were frosted cheeks? A bit painful, that was all; they were never serious.

Empty as the man's mind was of thoughts, he was keenly observant, and he noticed the changes in the creek, the curves and bends and timber jams, and always he sharply noted where he placed his feet. Once, coming around a bend, he shied abruptly, like a startled horse, curved away from the place where he had been walking, and retreated several paces back along the trail. The creek he knew was frozen clear to the bottom—no creek could contain water in that arctic winter— but he knew also that there were springs that bubbled out from the hillsides and ran along under the snow and on top the ice of the creek. He knew that the coldest snaps never froze these springs, and he knew likewise their danger. They were traps. They hid pools of water under the snow that might be three inches deep, or three feet. Sometimes a skin of ice half an inch thick covered them, and in turn was covered by the snow.

Sometimes there were alternate layers of water and ice skin, so that when one broke through he kept on breaking through for a while, sometimes wetting himself to the waist.

That was why he had shied in such panic. He had felt the give under his feet and heard the crackle of a snow-hidden ice skin. And to get his feet wet in such a temperature meant trouble and danger. At the very least it meant delay, for he would be forced to stop and build a fire, and under its protection to bare his feet while he dried his socks and moccasins. He stood and studied the creek bed and its banks, and decided that the flow of water came from the right. He reflected awhile, rubbing his nose and cheeks, then skirted to the left, stepping gingerly and testing the footing for each step. Once clear of the danger, he took a fresh chew of tobacco and swung along at his four-mile gait.

In the course of the next two hours he came upon several similar traps. Usually the snow above the hidden pools had a sunken, candied appearance that advertised the danger. Once again, however, he had a close call; and once, suspecting danger, he compelled the dog to go on in front. The dog did not want to go. It hung back until the man shoved it forward, and then it went quickly across the white, unbroken surface. Suddenly it broke through, floundered to one side, and got away to firmer footing. It had wet its forefeet and legs, and almost immediately the water that clung to it turned to ice. It made quick efforts to lick the ice off its legs, then dropped down in the snow and began to bite out the ice that had formed between the toes. This was a matter of instinct. To permit the ice to remain would mean sore feet. It did not know this. It merely obeyed the mysterious prompting that arose from the deep crypts of its being. But the man knew, having achieved a judgment on the subject, and he removed the mitten from his right hand and helped tear out the ice particles. He did not expose his fingers more than a minute, and was astonished at the swift numbness that smote them. It certainly was cold. He pulled on the mitten hastily, and beat the hand savagely across his chest.

At twelve o'clock the day was at its brightest. Yet the sun was too far south on its winter journey to clear the horizon. The bulge of the earth intervened between it and Henderson Creek, where the man walked under a clear sky at noon and cast no shadow. At half-past twelve, to the minute, he arrived at the forks of the creek. He was pleased at the speed he had made. If he kept it up, he would certainly be with the boys by six. He unbuttoned his jacket and shirt and drew forth his lunch. The action consumed no more than a quarter of a minute, yet in that brief moment the numbness laid hold of the exposed fingers. He did not put the mitten on, but, instead, struck the fingers a dozen sharp smashes against his leg. Then he sat down on a snow-covered log to eat. The sting that followed upon the striking of his fingers against his leg ceased so quickly that he was startled. He had no chance to take a bite of biscuit. He struck the fingers repeatedly and returned them to the mitten, baring the other hand for the purpose of eating. He tried to take a mouthful, but the ice muzzle prevented. He had forgotten to build a fire and thaw out. He chuckled at his foolishness, and as he chuckled he noted the numbness creeping into the exposed fingers. Also, he noted that the stinging which had first come to his toes when he sat down was already passing away. He wondered whether the toes were warm or numb. He moved them inside the moccasins and decided that they were numb.

He pulled the mitten on hurriedly and stood up. He was a bit frightened. He stamped up and down until the stinging returned into the feet. It certainly was cold, was his thought. That man from Sulphur Creek had spoken the truth when telling how cold it sometimes got in the country. And he had laughed at him at the time! That showed one must not be too sure of things. There was no mistake about it, it *was* cold. He strode up and down, stamping his feet and threshing his arms, until reassured by the returning warmth. Then he got out matches and proceeded to make a fire. From the undergrowth, where high water of the previous spring had lodged a supply of seasoned twigs, he got his firewood. Working carefully from a small beginning, he soon had a roaring fire, over which he thawed the ice from his face and in the protection of which he ate his biscuits. For the moment the cold of space was outwitted. The dog took satisfaction in the fire, stretching out close enough for warmth and far enough away to escape being singed.

When the man had finished, he filled his pipe and took his comfortable time over a smoke. Then he pulled on his mittens, settled the ear flaps of his cap firmly about his ears, and took the creek trail up the left fork. The dog was disappointed and yearned back toward the fire. This man did not know cold. Possibly all the generations of his ancestry had been ignorant of cold, of real cold, of cold one hundred and seven degrees below freezing point. But the dog knew; all its ancestry knew, and it had inherited the knowledge. And it knew that it was not good to walk abroad in such fearful cold. It was the time to lie snug in a hole in the snow and wait for a curtain of cloud to be drawn across the face of outer space whence this cold came. On the other hand, there was no keen intimacy between the dog and the man. The one was the toil–slave of the other, and the only caresses it had ever received were the caresses of the whip–lash and of harsh and menacing throat–sounds that threatened the whip–lash. So the dog made no effort to communicate its apprehension to the man. It was not concerned in the welfare of the man; it was for its own sake that it yearned back toward the fire. But the man whistled, and spoke to it with the sound of whip–lashes, and the dog swung in at the man's heels and followed after.

The man took a chew of tobacco and proceeded to start a new amber beard. Also, his moist breath quickly powdered with white his mustache, eyebrows, and lashes. There did not seem to be so many springs on the left fork of the Henderson, and for half an hour the man saw no signs of any. And then it happened. At a place where there were no signs, where the soft, unbroken snow seemed to advertise solidity beneath, the man broke through. It was not deep. He wet himself halfway to the knees before he floundered out to the firm crust.

He was angry, and cursed his luck aloud. He had hoped to get into camp with the boys at six o'clock, and this would delay him an hour, for he would have to build a fire and dry out his footgear. This was imperative at that low temperature—he knew that much; and he turned aside to the bank, which he climbed. On top, tangled in the underbrush about the trunks of several small spruce trees, was a high-water deposit of dry firewood—sticks and twigs, principally, but also larger portions of seasoned branches and fine, dry, last year's grasses. He threw down several large pieces on top of the snow. This served for a foundation and prevented the young flame from drowning itself in the snow it otherwise would melt. The flame he got by touching a match to a small shred of birch bark that he took from his pocket. This burned even more readily than paper. Placing it on the foundation, he fed the young flame with wisps of dry grass and with the tiniest dry twigs.

He worked slowly and carefully, keenly aware of his danger. Gradually, as the flame grew stronger, he increased the size of the twigs with which he fed it. He squatted in the snow, pulling the twigs out from their entanglement in the brush and feeding directly to the flame. He knew there must be no failure. When it is seventy-five below zero, a man must not fail in his first attempt to build a fire—that is, if his feet are wet. If his feet are dry, and he fails, he can run along the trail for half a mile and restore his circulation. But the circulation of wet and freezing feet cannot be restored by running when it is seventy-five below. No matter how fast he runs, the wet feet will freeze the harder.

All this the man knew. The old-timer on Sulphur Creek had told him about it the previous fall, and now he was appreciating the advice. Already all sensation had gone out of his feet. To build the fire he had been forced to remove his mittens, and the fingers had quickly gone numb. His pace of four miles an hour had kept his heart pumping blood to the surface of his body and to all the extremities. But the instant he stopped, the action of the pump eased down. The cold of space smote the unprotected tip of the planet, and he, being on that unprotected tip, received the full force of the blow. The blood of his body recoiled before it. The blood was alive, like the dog, and like the dog it wanted to hide away and cover itself up from the fearful cold. So long as he walked four miles an hour, he pumped that blood, willy-nilly, to the surface; but now it ebbed away and sank down into the recesses of his body. The extremities were the first to feel its absence. His wet feet froze the faster, and his exposed fingers numbed the faster, though they had not yet begun to freeze. Nose and cheeks were already freezing, while the skin of all his body chilled as it lost its blood.

But he was safe. Toes and nose and cheeks would be only touched by the frost, for the fire was beginning to burn with strength. He was feeding it with twigs the size of his finger. In another minute he would be able to feed it with branches the size of his wrist, and then he could remove his wet footgear, and, while it dried, he could keep his naked feet warm by the fire, rubbing them at first, of course, with snow. The fire was a success. He was safe. He remembered the advice of the old-timer on Sulphur Creek, and smiled. The old-timer had been very serious in laying down the law that no man must travel alone in the Klondike after fifty below. Well, here he was; he had had the accident; he was alone; and he had saved himself. Those old-timers were rather womanish, some of them, he thought. All a man had to do was to keep his head, and he was all right. Any man who was a man could travel alone. But it was surprising, the rapidity with which his cheeks and nose were freezing. And he had not thought his fingers could go lifeless in so short a time. Lifeless they were, for he could scarcely make them move together to grip a twig, and they seemed remote from his body and from him. When he touched a twig, he had to look and see whether or not he had hold of it.

The wires were pretty well down between him and his finger ends.

All of which counted for little. There was the fire, snapping and crackling and promising life with every dancing flame. He started to untie his moccasins. They were coated with ice; the thick German socks were like sheaths of iron halfway to the knees; and the moccasin strings were like rods of steel all twisted and knotted as by some conflagration. For a moment he tugged with his numb fingers, then, realizing the folly of it, he drew his sheath knife.

But before he could cut the strings, it happened. It was his own fault or, rather, his mistake. He should not have built the fire under the spruce tree. He should have built it in the open. But it had been easier to pull the twigs from the brush and drop them directly on the fire. Now the tree under which he had done this carried a weight of snow on its boughs. No wind had blown for weeks, and each bough was fully freighted. Each time he had pulled a twig he had communicated a slight agitation to the tree—an imperceptible agitation, so far as he was concerned, but an agitation sufficient to bring about the disaster. High up in the tree one bough capsized its load of snow. This fell on the boughs beneath them, capsizing them. This process continued, spreading out and involving the whole tree. It grew like a avalanche, and it descended without warning upon the man and the fire, and the fire was blotted out! Where it had burned was a mantle of fresh and disordered snow.

The man was shocked. It was as though he had just heard his own sentence of death. For a moment he sat and stared at the spot where the fire had been. Then he grew very calm. Perhaps the old-timer on Sulphur Creek was right. If he had only had a trail mate he would have been in no danger now. The trail mate could have built the fire. Well, it was up to him to build the fire over again, and this second time there must be no failure. Even it he succeeded, he would most likely lose some toes. His feet must be badly frozen by now, and there would be some time before the second fire was ready.

Such were his thoughts, but he did not sit and think them. He was busy all the time they were passing through his mind. He made a new foundation for a fire, this time in the open, where no treacherous tree could blot it out. Next he gathered dry grasses and tiny twigs from the high-water flotsam. He could not bring his fingers together to pull them out, but he was able to gather them by the handful. In this way he got many rotten twigs and bits of green moss that were undesirable, but it was the best he could do. He worked methodically, even collecting an armful of the larger branches to be used later when the fire gathered strength. And all the while the dog sat and watched him, a certain yearning wistfulness in its eyes, for it looked upon him as the fire–provider, and the fire was slow in coming.

When all was ready, the man reached in his pocket for a second piece of birch bark. He knew the bark was there, and, though he could not feel it with his fingers, he could hear its crisp rustling as he fumbled for it. Try as he would, he could not clutch hold of it. And all the time, in his consciousness, was the knowledge that each instant his feet were freezing. This thought tended to put him in a panic, but he fought against it and kept calm. He pulled on his mittens with his teeth, and threshed his arms back and forth, beating his hands with all his might against his sides. He did this sitting down, and he stood up to do it; and all the while the dog sat in the snow, its wolf brush of a tail curled around warmly over its forefeet, its sharp wolf ears pricked forward intently as it watched the man. And the man, as he beat and threshed with his arms and hands, felt a great surge of envy as he regarded the creature that was warm and secure in its natural covering.

After a time he was aware of the first faraway signals of sensation in his beaten fingers. The faint tingling grew stronger till it evolved into a stinging ache that was excruciating, but which the man hailed with satisfaction. He stripped the mitten from his right hand and fetched forth the birch bark. The exposed fingers were quickly going numb again.

Next he brought out his bunch of sulphur matches. But the tremendous cold had already driven the life out of his fingers. In his effort to separate one match from the others, the whole bunch fell in the snow. He tried to pick it out of the snow, but failed. The dead fingers could neither touch nor clutch. He was very careful. He drove the thought of his freezing feet, and nose, and cheeks, out of his mind, devoting his whole soul to the matches. He watched, using the sense of vision in place of that of touch, and when he saw his fingers on each side the bunch, he closed them—that is, he willed to close them, for the wires were down, and the fingers did not obey. He pulled the mitten on the right hand, and beat it fiercely against his knee. Then, with both mittened hands, he scooped the bunch of matches, along with much snow, into his lap. Yet he was no better off.

After some manipulation he managed to get the bunch between the heels of his mittened hands. In this fashion he carried it to his mouth. The ice crackled and snapped when by a violent effort he opened his mouth. He drew the lower jaw in, curled the upper lip out of the way, and scraped the bunch with his upper teeth in order to separate a match. He succeeded in getting one, which he dropped on his lap. He was no better off. He could not pick it up. Then he devised a way. He picked it up in his teeth and scratched on his leg. Twenty times he scratched before he succeeded in lighting it. As it flamed he held it with his teeth to the birch bark. But the burning brimstone went up his nostrils and into his lungs, causing him to cough spasmodically. The match fell into the snow and went out.

The old-timer on Sulphur Creek was right, he thought in the moment of controlled despair that ensued: after fifty below, a man should travel with a partner. He beat his hands, but failed in exciting any sensation. Suddenly he bared both hands, removing the mittens with his teeth. He caught the whole bunch between the heels of his hands. His arm muscles not being frozen enabled him to press the hand heels tightly against the matches. Then he scratched the bunch along his leg. It flared into flames, seventy sulphur matches at once! There was no wind to blow them out. He kept his head to one side to escape the strangling fumes, and held the blazing bunch to the birch bark. As he so held it, he became aware of sensation in his hand. His flesh was burning. He could smell it. Deep down below the surface he could feel it. The sensation developed into pain that grew acute. And still he endured it, holding the flame of the matches clumsily to the bark that would not light readily because his own burning hands were in the way, absorbing most of the flame.

At last, when he could endure no more, he jerked his hands apart. The blazing matches fell sizzling into the snow, but the birch-bark was alight. He began laying dry grasses and the tiniest twigs on the flame. He could not pick and choose, for he had to lift the fuel between the heels of his hands. Small pieces of rotten wood and green moss clung to the twigs, and he bit them off as well as he could with his teeth. He cherished the flame carefully and awkwardly. It meant life, and it must not perish. The withdrawal of blood from the surface of his body now made him begin to shiver, and he grew more awkward. A large piece of green moss fell squarely on the little fire. He tried to poke it out with his fingers, but his shivering frame made him poke too far, and he disrupted the nucleus of the little fire, the burning grasses and tiny twigs separating and scattering. He tried to poke them together again, but in spite of the tenseness of the effort, his shivering got away with him, and the twigs were hopelessly scattered. Each twig gushed a puff of smoke and went out. The fire-provider had failed. As he looked apathetically about him, his eyes chanced on the dog, sitting cross the ruins of the fire from him, in the snow, making restless, hunching movements, slightly lifting one forefoot and then the other, shifting its weight back and forth on them with wistful eagerness.

The sight of the dog put a wild idea into his head. He remembered the tale of the man, caught in a blizzard, who killed a steer and crawled inside the carcass, and so was saved. He would kill the dog and bury his hands in the warm body until the numbness went out of them. Then he could build another fire. He spoke to the dog, calling it to him; but in his voice was a strange note of fear that frightened the animal, who had never known the man to speak in such way before. Something was the matter, and its suspicious nature sensed danger—it knew not what danger, but somewhere, somehow, in its brain arose an apprehension of the man. It flattened its ears down at the sound of the man's voice, and its restless, hunching movements and the liftings and shiftings of its forefeet became more pronounced; but it would not come to the man. He got on his hands and knees and crawled toward the dog. This unusual posture again excited suspicion, and the animal sidled mincingly away.

The man sat up in the snow for a moment and struggled for calmness. Then he pulled on his mittens, by means of his teeth, and got upon his feet. He glanced down at first in order to assure himself that he was really standing up, for the absence of sensation in his feet left him unrelated to the earth. His erect position in itself started to drive the webs of suspicion from the dog's mind; and when he spoke peremptorily, with the sound of whip–lashes in his voice, the dog rendered its customary allegiance and came to him. As it came within reaching distance, the man lost his control. His arms flashed out to the dog, and he experienced genuine surprise when he discovered that his hands could not clutch, that there was neither bend nor feeling in the fingers. He had forgotten for the moment that they were frozen and that they were freezing more and more. All this happened quickly, and before the animal could get away, he encircled its body with his arms. He sat down in the snow, and in this fashion held the dog, while it snarled and whined and struggled.

But it was all he could do, hold its body encircled in his arms and sit there. He realized that he could not kill the dog. There was no way to do it. With his helpless hands he could neither draw nor hold his sheath knife nor throttle the animal. He released it, and it plunged wildly away, with tail between its legs, and still snarling. It halted forty feet away and surveyed him curiously, with ears sharply pricked forward.

The man looked down at his hands in order to locate them, and found them hanging on the ends of his arms. It struck him as curious that one should have to use his eyes in order to find out where his hands were. He began threshing his arms back and forth, beating the mittened hands against this sides. He did this for five minutes, violently, and his heart pumped enough blood up to the surface to put a stop to his shivering. But no sensation was aroused in the hands. He had an impression that they hung like weights on the ends of his arms, but when he tried to run the impression down, he could not find it.

A certain fear of death, dull and oppressive, came to him. This fear quickly became poignant as he realized that it was no longer a mere matter of freezing his fingers and toes, or of losing his hands and feet, but that it was a matter of life and death with the chances against him. This threw him into a panic, and he turned and ran up the creek bed along the old, dim trail. The dog joined in behind and kept up with him. He ran blindly, without intention, in fear such as he had never known in his life. Slowly, as he plowed and floundered through the snow, he began to see things again,—the banks of the creek, the old timber jams, the leafless aspens, and the sky. The running made him feel better. He did not shiver. Maybe, if he ran on, his feet would thaw out; and, anyway, if he ran far enough, he would reach camp and the boys. Without doubt he would lose some fingers and toes and some of his face; but the boys would take care of him, and save the rest of him when he got there. And at the same time there was another thought in his mind that said he would never get to the camp and the boys; that it was too many miles away, that the freezing had too great a start on him, and that he would soon be stiff and dead. This thought he kept in the background and refused to consider. Sometimes it pushed itself forward and demanded to be heard, but he thrust it back and strove to think of other things.

It struck him as curious that he could run at all on feet so frozen that he could not feel them when they struck the earth and took the weight of his body. He seemed to himself to skim along above the surface, and to have no connection with the earth. Somewhere he had once seen a winged Mercury, and he wondered if Mercury felt as he felt when skimming over the earth.

His theory of running until he reached camp and the boys had one flaw in it; he lacked the endurance. Several times he stumbled, and finally he tottered, crumpled up, and fell. When he tried to rise, he failed. He must sit and rest, he decided, and next time he would merely walk and keep on going. As he sat and regained his breath, he noted that he was feeling quite warm and comfortable. He was not shivering, and it even seemed that a warm glow had come to his chest and trunk. And yet, when he touched his nose or cheeks, there was no sensation. Running would not thaw them out. Nor would it thaw out his hands and feet. Then the thought came to him that the frozen portions of his body must be extending. He tried to keep this thought down, to forget it, to think of something else; he was aware of the panicky feeling that it caused, and he was afraid of the panic. But the thought asserted itself, and persisted, until it produced a vision of his body totally frozen. This was too much, and he made another wild run along the trail. Once he slowed down to a walk, but the thought of the freezing extending itself made him run again.

And all the time the dog ran with him, at his heels. When he fell down a second time, it curled its tail over its forefeet and sat in front of him, facing him, curiously eager and intent. The warmth and security of the animal angered him, and he cursed it until it flattened down its ears appeasingly. This time the shivering came more quickly upon the man. He was losing in his battle with the frost. It was creeping into his body from all sides. The thought of it drove him on, but he ran no more than a hundred feet, when he staggered and pitched headlong. It was his last panic. When he had recovered his breath and control, he sat up and entertained in his mind the conception of meeting death with dignity. However, the conception did not come to him in such terms. His idea of it was that he had been making a fool of himself, running around like a chicken with its head cut off—such was the simile that occurred to him. Well, he was bound to freeze anyway, and he might as well take it decently. With this new-found peace of mind came the first glimmerings of drowsiness. A good idea, he thought, to sleep off to death. It was like taking an anesthetic. Freezing was not so bad as people thought. There were lots worse ways to die.

He pictured the boys finding his body next day. Suddenly he found himself with them, coming along the trail and looking for himself. And, still with them, he came around a turn in the trail and found himself lying in the snow. He did not belong with himself any more, for even then he was out of himself, standing with the boys and looking at himself in the snow. It certainly was cold, was his thought. When he got back to the States he could tell the folks what real cold was. He drifted on from this to a vision of the old-timer on Sulphur Creek. He could see him quite clearly, warm and comfortable, and smoking a pipe.

"You were right, old hoss; you were right," the man mumbled to the old-timer of Sulphur Creek.

Then the man drowsed off into what seemed to him the most comfortable and satisfying sleep he had ever known. The dog sat facing him and waiting. The brief day drew to a close in a long, slow twilight. There were no signs of a fire to be made, and, besides, never in the dog's experience had it known a man to sit like that in the snow and make no fire. As the twilight drew on, its eager yearning for the fire mastered it, and with a great lifting and shifting of forefeet, it whined softly, then flattened its ears down in anticipation of being chidden by the man. But the man remained silent. Later the dog whined loudly. And still later it crept close to the man and caught the scent of death. This made the animal bristle and back away. A little longer it delayed, howling under the stars that leaped and danced and shown brightly in the cold sky. Then it turned and trotted up the trail in the direction of the camp it knew, where were the other food–providers and fire–providers.

---

1. In the story's beginning, what do we learn that could give the man trouble later?

2. The author tells about the bubbling springs of water hidden underneath the snow. How do the springs contribute to the conflict between the man and the Arctic?

3. What happens to the man which provides the turning point in the story?

4. The man is seized by fear and panic near the end of the story. After this climax, what is said to alert us that the action is slowing down?

5. What information did the man in the story have as he started on his journey, that might have saved his life had he paid attention to it?

6. The man in the story makes a sexist remark about the old timers. What was it? Given this attitude what did he do that eventually cost him his life? What attitude might have saved his life?

7. If you had the information that the man in the story had would you have made the same choices? What would you have done differently?

8. What role does the dog play in this story?

Choose one of the following topics to explore in a completely developed essay.

A. One of the outstanding features of "To Build a Fire" is the magnificent descriptions of the Yukon world well known by Jack London. The man in this story found out what "real cold was." Examine London's story and pick out the details that create the story's picture of the environment, one that defeats the man, but not the dog. After listing the details, explain the role of the Yukon Territory in the story.

B. We can all be foolish at times. When we fail to explore paths we don't clearly understand and prepare for in advance, our dreams can be destroyed. Choose one of your goals and show in your essay how you plan to move forward to reach that goal. Be aware of the obstacles in your path and be realistic. Also, realize that with time, other goals may become more important as we do change with new experiences. As the text states, proceed one step at a time, with your eyes open. Include what your present goal, once attained, could lead to.

C. Word choice is extremely important in writing. Good choices lead to clearer and more concise writing. Examine the story and find the key words which build the story. Does London repeat certain words? Are there certain phrases that set the scene as man travels toward his destination? What emotional atmosphere is created here?

Observational Writing

Read "Features of Observational Writing" and then write a description of a place that you know well, one that you can visualize in your mind with clarity. Bring this place to life on paper. Show how you feel about the special place in your description. Pick details with care, use sensory detail.

Features of Observational Writing

The following are important components in the techniques of observational writing. Try to incorporate these elements into your paper.

1. Word choice is important: carefully select words to describe your subject and maintain the stance.

2. Use specific concrete language. Sensory detail will serve to develop your description.

3. Vary the structure of your sentences.

4. You may use figurative language to illuminate your subject.

5. Use your imagination, make it vivid, try to take the reader there.

Jack London 1876–1916

Jack London was born in San Francisco in 1876 into extreme poverty. He dropped out of school to support his family and he became a sailor on a seal hunting ship, traveling to Japan and Siberia. The expeditions were exciting, and London thrived on adventure, but he also missed his youth. He began to turn his life around after being arrested for vagrancy in Buffalo, New York. He decided to complete his high school education and went on to college. During the gold rush of 1897, London mined in the Yukon Territory in Canada. He didn't strike it rich, and returned home with only $4.50 in gold dust in his pocket. London wasn't discouraged, instead he was inspired by life in the frozen country to write the American classics, *The Call of the Wild, The Sea-Wolf* and *White Fang*. Many of London's best works depict a person's struggle for survival against the powerful forces of nature. During the course of his career, he produced more than fifty books and earned more than a million dollars. His best known works are about men and animals who live in the wilderness. By 1912, London had become the best paid writer in the world; he was not happy, however. Addicted to drugs and alcohol, he died three years later of an overdose.

Journal entry:
> Some people believe that life is an uphill struggle. Do you agree or disagree?

Uphill

by Christina Rossetti

Does the road wind uphill all the way?
> Yes, to the very end.
Will the day's journey take the whole long day?
> From morn to night, my friend.

But is there for the night a resting place?
> A roof for when the slow dark hours begin.
May not the darkness hide it from my face?
> You cannot miss that inn.

Shall I meet other wayfarers at night?
> Those who have gone before.
Then must I knock, or call when just in sight?
> They will not keep you standing at that door.

Shall I find comfort, travel-sore and weak?
> Of labor you shall find the sum.
Will there be beds for me and all who seek?
> Yea, beds for all who come.

1. There are four lines in each stanza. Which lines are the questions and which lines are the answers?

2. Who is asking the questions?

3. Who is answering the questions?

4. What could the journey symbolize?

5. What could the road winding uphill stand for?

6. Why is the journey "uphill all the way"?

7. Where or what is the inn? When life has been difficult for you, has there been an inn? Do you think anyone has ever considered you an "inn"? When? What were the circumstances?

8. M. Scott Peck states in his best selling book, *The Road Less Traveled*: "Life is difficult . . . . Once we truly know that life is difficult—once we truly understand and accept it— then life is no longer difficult."

   Do you agree with this statement? Interview three to five adults from different generations. Do they agree with this statement? Can you think of a situation in your life where this philosophy would have been helpful?

9. Peck goes on to state: "Life is a series of problems. Do we moan about them or solve them?"

   Read pages 183 and 184 in *Career Choices* for an overview of Peck's problem solving techniques. Think about something right now that makes your life seem like it is all "uphill." Using Peck's technique, outline a strategy for solving your problem.

Journal entry:
> Have you ever had to complete a task that seemed so difficult that you thought it would never end? When you take on a task or problem, how important is it to see the rewards of your labor? In pairs, discuss what the task was and how you felt about it. Did you finally complete it? If you didn't, explain why you decided to quit and how it felt.

The Myth of Sisyphus
by Albert Camus

The gods had condemned Sisyphus to ceaselessly rolling a rock to the top of a mountain, whence the stone would fall back of its own weight. They had thought with some reason that there is no more dreadful punishment than futile and hopeless labor.

If one believes Homer, Sisyphus was the wisest and most prudent of mortals. According to another tradition, however, he was disposed to practice the profession of highwayman. I see no contradiction in this. Opinions differ as to the reasons why he became the futile laborer of the underworld. To begin with, he is accused of a certain levity in regard to the gods. He stole their secrets. Aegina, the daughter of Aesopus, was carried off by Jupiter. The father was shocked by that disappearance and complained to Sisyphus. He, who knew of the abduction, offered to tell about it on condition that Aesopus would give water to the citadel of Corinth. To the celestial thunderbolts he preferred the benediction of water. He was punished for this in the underworld. Homer tells us also that Sisyphus had put

Death in chains. Pluto could not endure the sight of his deserted, silent empire. He dispatched the god of war, who liberated Death from the hands of her conqueror.

It is said also that Sisyphus, being near to death, rashly wanted to test his wife's love. He ordered her to cast his unburied body into the middle of the public square. Sisyphus woke up in the underworld. And there, by an obedience so contrary to human love, he obtained from Pluto permission to return to earth in order to chastise his wife. But when he had seen again the face of this world, enjoyed water and sun, warm stones and the sea, he no longer wanted to go back to the infernal darkness. Recalls, signs of anger, warnings were of no avail. Many years more he lived facing the curve of gulf, the sparkling sea, and the smiles of earth. A decree of the gods was necessary. Mercury came and seized the impudent man by the collar and, snatching him from his joys, led him forcibly back to the underworld, where his rock was ready for him.

You have already grasped that Sisyphus is the absurd hero. He *is*, as much through his passions as through his torture. His scorn of the gods, his hatred of death, and his passion for life won him that unspeakable penalty in which the whole being is exerted toward accomplishing nothing. This is the price that must be paid for the passion of this earth.

Nothing is told us about Sisyphus in the underworld. Myths are made for the imagination to breathe life into them. As for this myth, one sees merely the whole effort of a body straining to raise the huge stone, roll it and push it up a slope a hundred times over; one sees the face screwed up, the cheek tight against the stone, the shoulder bracing the claycovered mass, the foot wedging it, the fresh start with arms outstretched, the wholly human security of two earth-clotted hands. At the very end of his long effort measured by skyless space and time without depth, the purpose is achieved. Then Sisyphus watches the stone rush down in a few moments toward that lower world whence he will have to push it up again toward the summit. He goes back down to the plain.

It is during that return, that pause, that Sisyphus interests me. A face that toils so close to stones is already stone itself! I see that man going back down with a heavy yet measured step toward the torment of which he will never know the end. That hour like a breathing-space which returns as surely as his suffering, that is the hour of consciousness. At each of those moments when he leaves the heights and gradually sinks toward the lairs of the gods, he is superior to his fate. He is stronger than his rock.

If this myth is tragic, that is because its hero is conscious. Where would his torture be, indeed, if at every step the hope of succeeding upheld him? The workman of today works every day of his life at the same tasks, and this fate is no less absurd. But it is tragic only at the rare moments when it becomes conscious. Sisyphus, proletarian of the gods, powerless and rebellious, knows the whole extent of his wretched condition: it is what he thinks of during his descent. The lucidity that was to constitute his torture at the same time crowns his victory. There is no fate that cannot be surmounted by scorn. If the descent is thus sometimes performed in sorrow, it can also take place in joy. This word is not too much. Again I fancy Sisyphus returning toward his rock, and the sorrow was in the beginning. When the images of earth cling too tightly to memory, when the call of happiness becomes too insistent, it happens that melancholy rises in man's heart: this is the rock's victory, this is the rock itself. The boundless grief is too heavy to bear. These are our nights of Gethsemane. But crushing truths perish from being acknowledged. Thus, Oedipus at the outset obeys fate without knowing it. But from the moment he knows, his tragedy begins. Yet at the same moment, blind and desperate, he realizes that the only bond linking him to the world is the cool hand of a girl. Then a tremendous remark rings out: "Despite so many ordeals, my advanced age and the nobility of my soul make me conclude that all is well." Sophocles' Oedipus, like Dostoevsky's Kirilov, thus gives the recipe for the absurd victory. Ancient wisdom confirms modern heroism.

One does not discover the absurd without being tempted to write a manual of happiness. "What! by such narrow ways—?" There is but one world, however. Happiness and the absurd are two sons of the same earth. They are inseparable. It would be a mistake to say that happiness necessarily springs from the absurd discovery. It happens as well that the feeling of the absurd springs from happiness. "I conclude that all is well," says Oedipus, and that remark is sacred. It echoes in the wild and limited universe of man. It teaches that all is not, has not been, exhausted. It drives out of this world a god who had come into it with dissatisfaction and a preference for futile sufferings. It makes of fate a human matter, which must be settled among men.

All Sisyphus' silent joy is contained therein. His fate belongs to him. His rock is his thing. Likewise, the absurd man, when he contemplates his torment, silences all the idols. In the universe suddenly restored to its silence, the myriad wondering little voices of the earth rise up. Unconscious, secret calls, invitations from all the faces, they are the necessary reverse and price of victory. There is no sun without shadow, and it is essential to know the night. The absurd man says yes and his effort will henceforth be unceasing. If there is a personal fate, there is no higher destiny, or at least there is but one which he concludes is inevitable and despicable. For the rest, he knows himself to be the master of his days. At that subtle moment when man glances backward over his life, Sisyphus returning toward his rock, in that slight pivoting he contemplates that series of unrelated actions which becomes his fate, created by him, combined under his memory's eye and soon sealed by his death. Thus, convinced of the wholly human origin of all that is human, a blind man eager to see who knows that the night has no end, he is still on the go. The rock is still rolling.

I leave Sisyphus at the foot of the mountain! One always finds one's burden again. But Sisyphus teaches the higher fidelity that negates the gods and raises rocks. He too concludes that all is well. This universe henceforth without a master seems to him neither sterile nor futile. Each atom of that stone, each mineral flake of that night-filled mountain, in itself forms a world. The struggle itself toward the heights is enough to fill a man's heart. One must imagine Sisyphus happy.

---

1. To what eternal punishment was Sisyphus condemned?

2. Explain what this could mean: There is "no more dreadful punishment than futile and hopeless labor." Did Camus agree?

3. Interpret what Camus meant when he wrote: "There is no sun without shadow, and it is essential to know the night."

4. Think about the problems or tasks you've dealt with during the last few years. Can you draw any parallels between your situation and Sisyphus' fate? Any contrast?

5. Does Camus believe that this myth is tragic? "Where would his torture be indeed, if at every step the hope of succeeding upheld him?" How important is it to you to have a sense of accomplishment when you are deciding whether or not to continue working on a difficult problem or task?

6. Write an essay comparing Sisyphus' walk down the hill with the weekend of the average American worker.

Interior Monologue

An interior monologue is a discussion that we have with ourselves. We constantly discuss and debate issues in conversations that take place only in our mind. To write an interior monologue is to show that thinking on paper.

"Myths are made for the imagination to breathe life into them." Breathe life into this myth. Pretend that you are Sisyphus. What would you be thinking as you pushed the stone up the mountain only to have it roll down again? Write that interior monologue.

Albert Camus 1913–1960

Albert Camus, was born in Mondovi, Algeria. He grew up in Northern Africa before moving to France as a journalist. In 1942 he published the philosophical essay, *The Myth of Sisyphus* and the novel *The Stranger* and these works brought him to the attention of intellectual circles. He published essays, novels, plays, and dramatic adaptations. Three of his most widely praised works of fiction were *The Plague*, *The Fall*, and *The Exile and The Kingdom*. In 1957 Camus was awarded the Nobel Prize for Literature. He was killed in an automobile accident in 1960.

Journal entry:
> What does the word "hope" mean to you? Ask your
> classmates to share their definition of the word "hope"
> with you. How is the word hope defined in the diction-
> ary?

Hope

by Emily Dickinson

"Hope" is the thing with feathers–
That perches in the soul–
And sings the tune without the words–
And never stops– at all–

And sweetest– in the Gale– is heard–
And sore must be the storm–
That could abash the little Bird
That kept so many warm–

I've heard it in the chillest land–
And on the strangest Sea–
Yet, never, in Extremity,
It asked a crumb– of Me.

1. Examine the first stanza of Emily Dickinson's poem. What "perches in the soul"? What does it sing? When does it stop?

2. Where has the poet heard the "little bird"? What has it never done?

3. Emily Dickinson employed a powerful metaphor in this poem when she compared the little bird to hope. What qualities does the bird possess? What is she saying about the nature of hope?

4. What does the last stanza suggest?

5. What does this poem suggest about the human spirit and it's ability to prevail? (Review Faulkner's speech.)

6. Why is it important to have hope?

7. Hope is a feeling sometimes described as "even the slightest possible, wonderful chance!" What possible, wonderful chance makes your stomach do little flips and keeps you trying?

8. List five synonyms and five antonyms for the word hope.

Emily Dickinson 1830–1886

Emily Dickinson was born in Amherst, Massachusetts, the daughter of a prominent lawyer. Although she travelled when she was young, she rarely left her home town as she grew older. During the last ten years of her life, she never left her house and garden. As her world grew smaller and smaller, she communicated with friends through notes and poems. The "Belle of Amherst" wore only white and wouldn't allow strangers or neighbors to see her. During her lifetime, Emily Dickinson wrote at least 1775 poems. Only seven of those were published, and those were published anonymously. The extent of her talent was not revealed until 1955 when a complete unedited edition of her poems was published. For the first time, her style, concrete imagery, and simple language was appreciated. Dickinson's work was compared with that of modern poets and was truly ahead of its time.

Journal entry:
> When waiting for something good to happen, have you ever found yourself saying, "Now, don't get your hopes up." Try and remember when you said that to someone or thought it to yourself. Why would you say something like that? What purpose would it serve?

Expect Nothing

by Alice Walker

Expect nothing. Live frugally
On surprise.
Become a stranger
To need of pity
Or, if compassion be freely
Given out
Take only enough
Stop short of urge to plead
Then purge away the need.

Wish for nothing larger
Than your own small heart

Or greater than a star:
Tame wild disappointment
With caress unmoved and cold
Make of it a parka
For your soul.

Continued

Discover the reason why
So tiny human midget
Exists at all
So scared unwise
But expect nothing. Live frugally
On surprise.

---

1. Summarize the theme of the poem.

2. The image of "greater than a star" doesn't seem to fit. Why do you suppose Walker chose this image?

3. Why do you think the author challenges you to . . . "discover the reason why so tiny human midget exists at all . . . ?"

4. What can we guess about the author of this poem? What is her point of view about life? What experiences might have lead her to that point of view?

5. With classmates, brainstorm situations in which the wisest strategy might be to, "Expect nothing. Live frugally on surprise."

6. What are the differences and similarities between the poems "Hope" by Emily Dickinson and "Expect Nothing" by Alice Walker?

7. If Alice Walker and Emily Dickinson met, what kind of conversation would they have? What things would they agree upon? On which topics would they be likely to disagree?

Alice Walker 1944–

Alice Walker was born in 1944, into a family of sharecroppers in Georgia. She is known for her fiction and poetry, and many of her themes deal with the plight of the African American woman. Her first book of poetry, *Once*, published in 1968, was inspired by a trip to Africa. After writing her second book of poetry, *Revolutionary Petunias and Other Poems*, Walker focused on writing fiction. Her first novel, *Meridian* (1976) was one of the finest novels to come out of the civil rights movement. Walker's third novel, *The Color Purple* (1982) earned a Pulitzer Prize.

Journal entry:

Have you ever felt so strongly about an injustice that you would consider breaking the law in order to correct it? Explain thoroughly. Can you think of a situation in the history of our country when people broke the law to try to correct an injustice? What did they do and why did they do it? What was the eventual outcome?

As you read this excerpt, note the areas where you can visualize the scene well, where the action seems to spring to life on the page.

from *The Prince of Tides*

by Pat Conroy

Chapter 16

It was almost summer when the strangers arrived by boat in Colleton and began their long, inexorable pursuit of the white porpoise. My mother was baking bread and the suffusion of that exquisite fragrance of the loaves and roses turned our house into a vial of the most harmonious seasonal incense. She took the bread fresh from the oven, then slathered it with butter and honey. We took it steaming in our hand, down to the dock to eat, the buttery honey running through our fingers. We attracted the ornery attention of every yellow jacket in our yard, and it took nerve to let them walk on our hands, gorging themselves on the drippings from our bread. They turned our hands into gardens and orchards and hives. My mother brought the lid of a mayonnaise jar full of sugar water down to the dock to appease the yellow jackets and let us eat in peace.

We had almost finished the bread when we saw the boat,

The Amberjack, bearing Florida registry, move through the channels of the Colleton River. No gulls followed the boat, so we were certain it was not a fishing vessel. It lacked the clean, luxurious lines of a yacht, yet there was a visible crew of six men whose sun-stained burnt-amber color announced them as veteran mariners. We would learn the same day that it was the first boat ever to enter South Carolina waters whose function was to keep fish alive.

The crew of *The Amberjack* were not secretive about their mission and their business in these waters was known all over Colleton later that afternoon. Captain Otto Blair told a reporter from the *Gazette* that the Miami Seaquarium had received a letter from a Colleton citizen, who wished to remain anonymous, that an albino porpoise frequented the waters around Colleton. Captain Blair and his crew planned to capture the porpoise, then transport it back to Miami, where it would be both a tourist attraction and a subject for scientific inquiry. The crew of *The Amberjack* had come to Colleton in the interest of science, as marine biologists, inspired by a report that the rarest creature in the seven seas was a daily sight to the people of the lowcountry.

They may have known all there was to know about porpoises and their habits, but they had badly misjudged the character of the people they would find in the lower part of South Carolina. The citizens of Colleton were about to give them lessons free of charge. A collective shiver of rage passed invisibly through Colleton; the town was watchful and alarmed. The plot to steal Carolina Snow was an aberrant, unspeakable act to us. By accident, they had brought the rare savor of solidarity to our shores. They would feel the full weight of our dissent.

To them the white porpoise was a curiosity of science; to us she was the disclosure of the unutterable beauty and generosity of God among us, the proof of magic, and the ecstasy of art.

The white porpoise was something worthy to fight for.

The Amberjack, mimicking the habits of the shrimpers, moved out early the next morning, but it did not sight the porpoise that day and it set no nets. The men returned to the shrimp dock grim-lipped and eager for rumors about recent sightings of the Snow. They were met with silence.

After the third day, Luke and I met their boat and listened to the crew talk about the long fruitless days on the river, trying to sight the white porpoise. Already, they were feeling the eloquent heft of the town's censure and they seemed eager to talk to Luke and me, to extract any information about the porpoise they could from us.

Captain Blair brought Luke and me on board *The Amberjack* and showed us the holding tank on the main deck where specimens were kept alive until they could reach the aquariums in Miami. He showed us the half mile of nets that they would use to encircle the porpoise. A man's hand could pass easily through the meshing of their nets. The captain was a cordial middle-aged man and the sun had burned deep lines in his face, like tread marks. In a soft, barely discernible voice he told us how they trained a porpoise to eat dead fish after a capture. A porpoise would fast for two weeks or more before it would deign to feed on prey it would ignore in the wild. The greatest danger in the capture of a porpoise was that the animal would become entangled in the nets and drown. Hunting dolphins required a swift and skilled crew to ensure that drowning did not occur. He then showed us the foam rubber mattresses they laid the porpoises on once they got them on board.

"Why don't you just throw them in the pool, Captain?" I asked.

"We do usually, but sometimes we've got sharks in the pool and sometimes a porpoise will hurt himself thrashing around in a pool that small. Often it's better to just lie 'em down on these mattresses and keep splashing 'em with seawater so their skin won't dry out. We move 'em from side to side to keep their circulation right and that's about all there is to it."

"How long can they live out of the water?" Luke asked.

"I don't rightly know, son," the captain answered. "The longest I ever kept one out of the water was five days, but he made it back to Miami just fine. They're hardy creatures. When's the last time you boys spotted Moby in these waters?"

"Moby?" Luke said. "Her name is Snow. Carolina Snow."

"That's what they've named her down at Miami, boys. Moby Porpoise. Some guy in the publicity department came up with that one."

"That's the dumbest name I've ever heard," Luke said.

"It'll bring the tourists running, son," Captain Blair answered.

"Speaking of tourists, a whole boatful spotted the Snow yesterday morning in Charleston Harbor as they were heading out for Fort Sumter, " said Luke.

"Are you sure, son?" the captain asked, and one of the crewmen leapt to his feet to hear the rest of the conversation.

"I didn't see it," Luke said, "but I heard it on the radio."

The Amberjack left for Charleston Harbor the next day, cruising the Ashley and the Cooper rivers looking for signs of the white porpoise. For three days they searched the waters around Wappoo Creek and the Elliott Cut before they realized that my brother Luke was a liar. They had also taught my brother how to keep a porpoise alive if the need ever arose.

The call to arms between *The Amberjack* crew and the town did not begin in earnest until the evening in June when the crew tried to capture the white porpoise in full view of the town. They had sighted the Snow in Colleton Sound, in water much too deep to set their nets for a successful capture. All day, they had followed the porpoise, remaining a discreet distance behind her, stalking her with infinite patience until she began moving into the shallower rivers and creeks.

Just as the crew tracked the porpoise, the shrimpers of the town kept issuing reports on the position of *The Amberjack* on their short-wave radios. Whenever the boat changed course, the eyes of the shrimp fleet noted and remarked upon the shift of position, and the airwaves filled up with the voices of shrimpers passing messages from boat to boat, from boat to town. The shrimpers' wives, monitoring their own radios, then got on the telephone to spread the news. *The Amberjack* could not move through county waters without its exact bearings being reported to a regiment of secret listeners.

"*Amberjack* turning into Yemassee Creek," we heard one day through the static of the radio my mother kept above the kitchen sink. "Don't look like they found any Snow today."

"Miami Beach just left Yemassee Creek and appears to be settin' to poke around the Harper Dogleg up by Goat Island."

The town carefully listened to these frequent intelligence reports of the shrimpers. For a week the white porpoise did not appear, and when she did it was one of the shrimpers who alerted the town.

"This is Captain Willard Plunkett and Miami Beach has got the Snow in sight. They are pursuing her up the Colleton River and the crew is preparing the nets on deck. It looks like Snow is heading for a visit to town."

Word passed through the town in the old quicksilvering of rumor, and the prefigured power of that rumor lured the whole town to the river's edge. People kept their eyes on the river and talked quietly. The sheriff pulled into the parking lot behind the bank and monitored the shrimpers' reports. The eyes of the town were fixed on the bend in the Colleton River where *The Amberjack* would make its appearance. That bend was a mile from the point where the river joined three of its sister rivers and bloomed into a sound.

For twenty minutes we waited for *The Amberjack* to make the turn, and when it did a collective groan rose up in the throats of us all. The boat was riding high above the marsh on an incoming tide. One of the crewmen stood on the foredeck with a pair of binoculars trained on the water in front of the boat. He stood perfectly still, rapt and statuesque, his complete immersion a testament to the passion he brought to his task.

Luke, Savannah, and I watched from the bridge, along with several hundred of our neighbors who had gathered to witness the moment of capture of the town's living symbol of good luck. The town was only curious until we saw Carolina Snow make her own luxurious appearance as she rounded the last curve of the river and began her silken, fabulous promenade through the town. She silvered as the sunlight caught her pale fin buttering through the crest of a small wave. In her movement through town she achieved a fragile sublimity, so unaware was she of her vulnerability. Burnished by perfect light, she dazzled us again with her complete and ambient beauty. Her dorsal fin broke the surface again like a white chevron a hundred yards nearer the bridge, and to our surprise, the town cheered spontaneously and the apotheosis of the white porpoise was fully achieved. The ensign of Colleton's wrath unfurled in the secret winds and our status as passive observers changed imperceptibly as a battle cry, unknown to any of us, formed on our lips. All the mottoes and passwords of engagement appeared like fiery graffiti on the armorial bearings of the town's unconscious. The porpoise disappeared again, then rose up, arcing toward the applause that greeted her sounding. She was mysterious and lunar. Her color was a delicate alchemy of lily and mother-of-pearl. The porpoise passed argentine beneath the sun-struck waters. Then we looked up and saw *The Amberjack* gaining ground on the Snow and the crew getting the nets into a small boat they were going to lower into the water.

The town needed a warrior and I was surprised to find him standing beside me.

Traffic jammed the bridge as drivers simply parked their cars and went to the bridge's railing to watch the capture of the porpoise. A truck loaded down with tomatoes from one of Reese Newbury's farms was stuck on the bridge and the driver was leaning on his horn in vain, trying to get the other drivers back into their cars.

I heard Luke whisper to himself, "No. It just ain't right,"

and he left my side and mounted the back of the truck and began to toss crates of tomatoes down among the crowd. I thought Luke had gone crazy, but suddenly I understood, and Savannah and I bashed a crate of tomatoes open and began to pass them along the railing. The driver got out and screamed for Luke to stop, but Luke ignored him and continued passing the wooden crates down to the outstretched arms of his friends and neighbors. The driver's voice grew more and more frantic as people began taking tire tools from their trunks and splitting the crates wide open. The sheriff's car moved out of the parking lot and headed out toward the Charleston highway on the opposite side of town.

When *The Amberjack* neared the bridge, two hundred tomatoes hit the deck in a green fusillade that put the man with the binoculars to his knees. The tomatoes were hard and green and one of the other crewmen working on the nets was holding his nose near the aft of the boat, blood leaking through his fingers. The second salvo of tomatoes followed soon afterward and the crew scrambled, dazed and insensible, toward the safety of the hold and cabin. A tire tool cracked against a lifeboat and the crowd roared its approval. Boxes of tomatoes were passed down the line, the driver still screaming and not a single soul listening to his pleadings.

The Amberjack disappeared beneath the bridge and two hundred people crossed to the other side in a delirious, headlong rush. When the boat reappeared we showered it with tomatoes again, like archers on high ground pouring arrows on an ill-deployed infantry. Savannah was throwing hard and with accuracy, finding her own good rhythm, her own style. She was screaming with pure pleasure. Luke threw a whole crate of tomatoes and it smashed on the rear deck, sending ruined tomatoes skittering like marbles toward the battened-down hold.

The Amberjack pulled out of range of all but the strongest arms when the porpoise, in a thoughtless gesture of self-preservation, reversed her course and turned back toward the town, passing the boat trailing her on its starboard side. She returned to our applause and our advocacy. We watched her move beneath the waters below the bridge, grizzling the bright waves like some abstract dream of ivory. When the boat made its long, hesitant turn in the river, even more crates of tomatoes were passed through the mob. By this time, even the truck driver had surrendered to whatever mass hysteria had possessed the rest of us and he stood with his arm cocked, holding a tomato, anticipating with the rest of us *The Amberjack's* imminent return. The boat started back for the bridge, then turned abruptly away from us and moved north on the Colleton River as Carolina Snow, the only white porpoise on our planet, moved back toward the Atlantic.

The next day the town council passed a resolution enfranchising Carolina Snow as a citizen of Colleton County and made it a felony for anyone to remove her from county waters. At the same time, the South Carolina state legislature passed a similar law rendering it a felony for anyone to remove genus *Phocaena* or genus *Tursiops* from the waters of Colleton County. In less than twenty-four hours, Colleton County became the only place in the world where it was a crime to capture a porpoise.

Captain Blair went straight to the sheriff's office when he reached the shrimp dock that night and demanded that Sheriff Lucas arrest everyone who had thrown a tomato at *The Amberjack*. Unfortunately, Captain Blair could not provide the sheriff with a single name of even one of the miscreants, and the sheriff, after making several phone calls, could produce four witnesses who would swear in a court of law that no one had been on the bridge when *The Amberjack* passed beneath it.

"Then how did I get a hundred pounds of tomatoes on the deck of my boat?" the captain had asked.

And in a laconic reply that was well received in each Colleton household, the sheriff had answered, "It's tomato season, Captain. Those damn things will grow anywhere."

But the men from Miami quickly recovered their will and developed a new plan for the capture of the porpoise. They kept out of sight of the town and did not enter the main channel of the Colleton River again. They began to haunt the outer territorial limits of the county, waiting for that perfect moment when the Snow would wander out of county waters and beyond the protection of those newly contracted laws. But *The Amberjack* was shadowed by boats from the South Carolina Game and Fish Commission and by a small flotilla of recreational boats commanded by the women and children of the town. Whenever The *Amberjack* picked up the trail of the porpoise, the small crafts would maneuver themselves between the porpoise and the pursuing vessel and slow their motors. *The Amberjack* would try to weave between the boats, but these women and children of Colleton had handled small boats all their lives. They would interfere with the Florida boat's progress until the white porpoise slipped away in the enfolding tides of Colleton Sound.

Each day Luke, Savannah, and I would take our boat and ride up the inland waterway to join the flotilla of resistance. Luke would move the boat in front of *The Amberjack's* bow, ignoring the warning horn, and slow the Whaler by imperceptible degrees. No matter how skillfully Captain Blair maneuvered his boat, he could not pass Luke. Savannah and I had our fishing gear rigged and we trolled for Spanish mackerel as Luke navigated between *The Amberjack* and the white porpoise. Often, the crew would come out to the bow of the ship to threaten and taunt us.

"Hey, kids, get out of our goddamn way before we get pissed off," one crewman yelled.

"Just fishing, mister," Luke would shoot back.

"What're you fishing for?" The man sneered in exasperation.

"We hear there's a white porpoise in these waters," said Luke, slowing the motor with a delicate movement of his wrist.

"Is that right, smartass? Well, you're not doing such a

good job catching it."

"We're doing as good as you are, mister," Luke answered pleasantly.

"If this were Florida, we'd run right over you."

"It ain't Florida, mister. Or haven't you noticed?" Luke said.

"Hicks," the man screamed.

Luke pulled back the throttle and we slowed almost to a crawl. We could hear the big engines of *The Amberjack* throttling down behind us as the bow of the boat loomed over us.

"He called us hicks," Luke said.

"Me, a hick?" Savannah said.

"That hurts my feelings," I said.

Up ahead, the white porpoise turned into Langford Creek, the alabaster shine in her fin disappearing behind a green flange of marsh. There were three boats waiting at the mouth of the creek ready to intercept *The Amberjack* if it managed to get past Luke.

After thirty days of delay and obstruction, *The Amberjack* left the southern boundaries of Colleton waters and returned to its home base of Miami without the white porpoise. Captain Blair gave a final embittered interview to the *Gazette*, listing the many obstacles the citizens of Colleton had erected to disrupt the mission of *The Amberjack*. Such deterrence, he said, could not be allowed to frustrate the integrity of scientific investigation. But on their last day, he and his crew had taken sniper fire from Freeman's Island and he, as captain, had made the irrevocable decision to discontinue the hunt. The shrimp fleet observed *The Amberjack* as it passed the last barrier islands, maneuvered through the breakers, then turned south, angling toward the open seas.

But *The Amberjack* did not go to Miami. It traveled south for forty miles, then turned into the mouth of the Savannah River, putting in to the shrimp dock at Thunderbolt. There it remained for a week to resupply and to let the passions in Colleton County cool, still monitoring the short-wave radio, following the travels of the white porpoise by listening to the Colleton shrimpers give accurate reports of her soundings. After a week *The Amberjack* left the harbor in Savannah in the middle of the night and turned north out beyond the three-mile limit. They cruised confidently out of sight of the shore-bound shrimp trawlers. They were waiting for one signal to come over the radio.

They had been offshore for three days when they heard the words they had been waiting for.

"There's a submerged log I just netted in Zajac Creek, shrimpers. You boys be careful if you're over this way. Out."

"There's no shrimp in Zajac Creek anyhow, Captain," a voice of another shrimp boat captain answered. "You a long way from home, Captain Henry? Out."

"I'll catch the shrimp wherever I can find them, Captain. Out," my father answered, watching Carolina Snow moving a school of fish toward a sandbar.

Zajac Creek was not in Colleton County and *The Amberjack* turned west and came at full throttle toward the creek, the crew preparing the nets as the shoreline of South Carolina filled the eyes of Captain Blair for the last time. A shrimper from Charleston witnessed the capture of the white porpoise at 1130 hours that morning, saw Carolina Snow panic and charge the encircling nets, saw when she entangled herself, and admired the swiftness and skill of the crew as they got their ropes around her, held her head above the water to keep her from drowning, and maneuvered her into one of the motorboats.

By the time the word reached Colleton, *The Amberjack* was well outside the three-mile limit again, set on a southerly course that would take them into Miami in fifty-eight hours. The bells of the church were rung in protest, an articulation of our impotence and fury. It was as if the river had been deconsecrated, purged of all the entitlements of magic.

"Submerged log" was the code phrase my father had worked out with Captain Blair and the crew of *The Amberjack*. He had agreed to fish the boundary waters at the edge of the county until he sighted the white porpoise moving into the territorial waters of Gibbes County to the north. My father was the anonymous Colletonian who had written the Miami Seaquarium informing them of the presence of an albino porpoise in our county. Two weeks after the abduction of Snow and a week after her picture appeared in the *Colleton Gazette* being lowered into her aquarium tank in her new Miami home, my father received a letter of gratitude from Captain Blair and a check for a thousand dollars as a reward for his assistance.

"I'm ashamed of what you did, Henry," my mother said, barely able to control her temper as my father waved the check in front of us.

"I earned a thousand big ones, Lila, and it was the easiest money I ever made in my life. I wish every porpoise I passed was an albino so I could spend all my time eating chocolate and buying banks."

"If anybody in this town had any guts, they'd go to Miami and set that animal free. You'd better not let anyone in town hear that you're responsible, Henry. Folks are still steaming mad about that porpoise."

"How could you sell our porpoise, Daddy?" Savannah asked.

"Look, sweetie, that porpoise is gonna be in fat city, chowing down on gourmet mackerel and jumping through hoops to make kids happy. Snow doesn't have to worry about a shark the rest of her life. She's retired in Miami. You got to look at it in a positive light."

"I think you've committed a sin that not even God can forgive, Daddy," Luke said darkly.

"You do?" My father sneered. "Hey, I never Saw 'Property of Colleton' tattooed on her back. I just wrote the Seaquarium that Colleton had a natural phenomenon that could lure in the crowds and they rewarded me for being on my toes."

"They couldn't have found him if you hadn't radioed every time you spotted him in the river," I said.

"I was their liaison officer in the area. Look, it's not that great a shrimping season. This thousand bucks is going to put food on the table and clothes on your back. This could pay for a whole year of college for one of you kids."

"I wouldn't eat a bite of food you bought with that money," Luke said. "And I wouldn't wear a pair of Jockey shorts you bought with it either."

"I've been watching the Snow for more than five years now," my mother said. "You once punished Tom for killing a bald eagle, Henry. There's a lot more eagles in the world than white porpoises."

"I didn't kill the porpoise, Lila. I delivered it to a safe harbor where it will be free of all fear. I look upon myself as the hero of this affair."

"You sold Snow into captivity," my mother said.

"They're going to make her a circus porpoise," Savannah added.

"You betrayed yourself and your sources," Luke said. "If it was a businessman, I could understand. Some low-life creepy Jaycee with shiny hair. But a shrimper, Dad. A shrimper selling Snow for money."

"I sell shrimp for money, Luke," my father shouted.

"Not the same," Luke said. "You don't sell what you can't replace."

"I saw twenty porpoises in the river today."

"And I promise you, Daddy, not one of them was white. None of them was special," Luke said.

"Our family is the reason they captured the Snow," said Savannah. "It's like being the daughter of Judas Iscariot, only I bet I'd have liked Judas a lot better."

"You shouldn't have done what you did, Henry," my mother said. "It'll bring bad luck."

"I couldn't have had any worse luck than I've had," my father answered. "Anyway, it's done. There's nothing anyone can do about it now."

"I can do something about it," said Luke.

Three weeks later, in the languorous starry dark, when my parents were asleep and we could hear the soft chaos of my father's snoring, Luke whispered a plan to us. It should not have surprised us, but years later, Savannah and I would talk and wonder about the exact hour when our older brother turned from a passionate, idealistic boy into a man of action. Both of us were terrified and exhilarated by the boldness of his proposal, but neither of us wanted any part of it. But Luke continued to urge us quietly until we found ourselves imprisoned by the magnetic originality of his gentle eloquence. His decision was already made and he spent half the night enlisting us as recruits in his first real dance on the wild side. Ever since the night we watched him facing the tiger alone in the barn, we had known Luke was brave, but now we were faced with the probability that Luke was also reckless.

Three mornings later, after Luke had made exhaustive preparations, we were on Highway 17, thundering south, with Luke stepping hard on the accelerator, and the radio turned up high. Ray Charles was singing "Hit the Road, Jack" and we were singing it along with him. We were drinking beer iced down in a cooler and had the radio tuned to the Big Ape in Jacksonville as we shot across the Eugene Talmadge Memorial Bridge in Savannah. We slowed up at the toll gate and Luke handed the old man who was doling out tickets a dollar for a round tripper.

"You gonna do a little shopping in Savannah, kids?" the old man asked.

"No, sir," Luke replied, "we're on our way to Florida to steal us a porpoise."

On that bizarre and headlong flight to Florida my senses blazed like five brilliant fires behind my eyes. I felt as if I could point at a palm tree and it would burst into flame. I was electric, charged, ecstatic, and terror-stricken. Each song that came on the radio sounded as though it were sung expressly for my pleasure. Though I have an execrable singing voice, I thought my singing was terrific as we stayed on the coastal highway and burned down the oak-lined Georgia roads with Luke changing gears only when we slowed down for towns. Speed was in Luke's blood and we crossed the Florida state line two hours after we had left Melrose Island, and we didn't even stop for a glass of free orange juice at the welcome station.

The city of Jacksonville slowed us up some, but the St. Johns River was a grand thing and the first river we had ever seen that flowed north. Once we hit Highway A1A we were blistering the asphalt again and the tires sang against the macadam and the ocean appeared in intervals to our left. As the warm wind rushed into the cab, we felt that the sea was racing south with us, aware of our mission, yes, aware and approving and partisan.

We rode south with larcenous hearts and the sensibilities of outlaws, feeding off one another's bewildered energy. I turned and saw Luke laughing at some remark that Savannah had made and I felt the flow of her long hair against my cheek and the sweet smell of that hair, and I filled up with a perfect, ineffable love of my brother and sister, a love so vivid and powerful I could taste it on my tongue and feel its glorious heat burn deeply in my chest. Leaning over, I kissed Savannah on the neck and I squeezed Luke's shoulder with my left hand. He reached up and squeezed my hand, then surprised me by taking my hand and bringing it to his lips in a gesture of surpassing tenderness. I leaned back and let the smell of the state of Florida flood my senses in the watery light of Sunday.

After ten hours of hard driving and two stops for gas, the city of Miami rose out of the sea as we drove past the sign for the Hialeah racetrack. Coconut palms rattled in the warm breezes and the scent of gardens overwhelmed by bougainvillea cologned the broad avenues. We had never been to

Florida in our lives and suddenly we were cruising the streets of Miami looking for a place to set our tents beneath the lime and avocado trees.

"What do we do now, Luke?" I asked. "We can't just walk up and say, 'Hello, we've driven down here to steal your white porpoise. Do you mind packing her bags?' "

"We look around," Luke answered. "We put our heads together. I got a preliminary plan. But we got to be prepared. First we case the joint. There's got to be a night watchman, some yo-yo who makes sure little kids don't sneak in at night to try and catch Flipper with a cane pole."

"What will we do about the night watchman?" Savannah asked.

"I don't want to have to kill him," said Luke evenly. "How about you two?"

"Are you crazy Luke?" I said. "Are you out of your god-damn tree?"

"That's just a contingency plan."

"No, it's not, Luke," said Savannah. "If that's a contingency plan, then we're not part of it."

"I was only joking. They've got a killer whale locked up in this place. We can check him out tomorrow too."

"We aren't rescuing the killer whale, Luke," Savannah said.

"I know that sound in your voice and the killer whale is out."

"Maybe we can set every fish in the whole goddamn place free," Luke said. "I mean, have a real breakout."

"Why do they call them killer whales?" I asked.

"I think they love to kick ass," Luke explained.

We took the causeway that led out toward Key Biscayne and passed the Seaquarium on our right. Luke slowed the truck as we drove through the parking lot, observing the single light that shone from a security man's office. He came to the window and looked out, his face framed by a corona of electric light, making him featureless and absurd. An eight-foot fence, topped with barbed wire, protected the compound from intruders. Luke gunned the engine and we scissored out of the parking lot, spitting gravel behind us. We knew we were going by the zoo when we passed a place on the road that smelled like Caesar's cage magnified a hundred times. An elephant trumpeted somewhere in the darkness and Luke answered him with a trumpeting of his own.

"That didn't sound like an elephant, Luke," Savannah said.

"I thought it was pretty good," Luke said. "What do you think it sounded like?"

"An oyster farting through Crisco," she answered.

Luke roared and put his arm around Savannah and hugged her to his chest. That night we slept on a bench at Key Biscayne and the sun was high when we arose the next morning, gathered our belongings, and headed for a visit to the Seaquarium.

We paid our admission fees and walked through the turnstiles. For the first half-hour we circumnavigated the park, following the parabola made by the large Cyclone fence and its ugly toupee of barbed wire. Beside a cluster of palms contiguous to the parking lot, Luke stopped and said, "I'll back the truck up to these trees and I'll cut a hole right through here."

"What if they catch us, Luke?" I asked.

"We're just high school kids from Colleton who came down to rescue Snow on a dare from our classmates. We act the total hicks and pretend the coolest thing we ever did was spit watermelon seeds at sheets hanging in our mama's back yard."

"The guard at the gate was wearing a gun, Luke," Savannah said.

"I know, honey, but no guard is going to shoot at us."

"How do you know?" she asked.

"Because Tolitha gave me a whole bottle of sleeping pills. You know, the ones she calls her little red devils."

"Do we just tell him to say 'ah' and pop a pill in his

mouth?" I said, fearing that Luke's master plan would prove a bit leaky in its execution.

"I haven't figured that out yet, little brother," Luke said. "I just found me the place where I'm going to cut the hole.

How we gonna get Snow out of the water?" I asked.

"Same way. Sleeping pills," he answered.

"That'll be easy," I said. "We'll just jump in the water, swim our asses off until we catch a porpoise that it took experts a month to catch when they had all the equipment in the world, and then slip a few sleeping pills between her lips. Great plan, Luke."

"More than a few pills, Tom. We've got to make damn sure that the Snow is completely tranquilized."

"This will be the first porpoise in history to die of a drug overdose," Savannah said.

"No, I figure the Snow weighs about four hundred pounds. Tolitha weighs a hundred pounds. She takes one pill every night. We'll give Snow four or five of the babies."

"Who ever heard of a porpoise taking sleeping pills, Luke?" Savannah said. "Tom's right."

"I haven't either," Luke admitted. "But I've heard of a porpoise eating fish. And if that fish just happens to be chock-full of sleeping pills, then it's my theory that porpoise will be ready for rock-a-bye-baby time."

I asked, "Do porpoises sleep, Luke?"

"I don't know," he answered. "We're going to find out a lot about porpoises on this little expedition, Tom."

"What if it doesn't work, Luke?" Savannah asked.

Luke shrugged his shoulders and said, "No harm in that, Savannah. At least we'll know we tried to do something. And ain't we had some fun so far? All those people in Colleton crying about losing their porpoise and you, me, and Tom down here in Miami planning the jailbreak. We'll tell our kids about it. If we manage to get Snow out of here, there'll be parades and confetti and riding in convertibles. We'll brag about it until the day we die. But first, you got to see it. Neither of you see it yet. Now that's real important. Here, I'll help you. Close your eyes. . . "

Savannah and I closed our eyes and listened to our brother's voice. "Okay. Tom and I have the porpoise in the water. We move her over to the place where Savannah is waiting with the stretcher. We get ropes around the Snow and very gently we roll her out of the water and tie her to the stretcher. The guard is asleep because we drugged his Pepsi a couple of hours before. See it? Can you visualize it? We get the porpoise in the pickup and we're off. And here's the important thing. Listen to this. We're standing in the boat landing in Colleton and we take the Snow and we untie the ropes and we set her free in the river where she was born and where she belongs. Can you see it? Can you see it all, Tom and Savannah?"

His voice was hypnotic, transported, and we both opened our eyes at the same time and we nodded toward each other. Both of us could see it.

We continued our long walk around the perimeter of the park and saw *The Amberjack* tied up at its berth at the south end of the Seaquarium. There was no sign of the crew around, but we avoided any approach to the boat. Turning toward the porpoise house, we crossed a wooden bridge suspended high over a deep clear moat where huge sharks moved sluggishly in an endless circle. The sharks swam at twenty-yard intervals and there was very little room or inclination for them to pass one another. We watched a hammerhead and a young mako make their torpid passage beneath us as the crowd watched with breathless wonder. So monotonous was the movement of their great tails, so proscribed was their freedom for improvisation or movement, that they seemed purged of all their ferocious grandeur. Beneath the gazes of tourists, they looked as docile and harmless as black mollies.

The crowd was large and good-natured and we followed a processional of Bermuda shorts and rubber-soled thongs toward the amphitheater where the killer whale, Dreadnought, would perform at noon. From our brief encounter, Florida seemed to be a place where amiable crowds met to display white shape-less arms and acres of sun-starved hairless legs. The sun had parched the grass to the palest of greens and automatic sprinkler systems worked the infields off the gravel paths and ruby-throated hummingbirds droned among the lilies. As we neared the amphitheater, we passed a sign that read, "Visit Moby Porpoise at feeding time."

"I think we will," Luke said.

We listened to the tourists talking about the white porpoise as they filed into the rows of seats that ringed a vast two-mil-lion-gallon tank aquarium. When we were all seated, a well-made blond boy with coppery shoulders walked out onto a wooden peninsula jutting out over the water and waved to the crowd. A woman announcer presented the history of Dread-nought, the killer whale who had been captured in a pod of twelve whales near Queen Charlotte Strait off Vancouver Island and flown to Miami by special flight. The Seaquarium had paid sixty thousand dollars for the purchase of Dreadnought and it had taken a year to train the killer whale. The whale could not be incorporated into the porpoise show because por-poise was a favorite food of *Orcinus orca*.

As she spoke, a gate opened invisibly underwater and the passage of something awesome roiled the opaque depths below.

The tanned boy peered into the water, seeing something rising up toward him. His platform was twenty feet above the surface and you could study the intensity of his concentration by counting the lines on his forehead as he leaned forward holding a Spanish mackerel by the tail. The boy made a cir-cling gesture with his hand and in obedience the water was suddenly runnelled with waves spun outward from the center of the aquarium. Then the whale went to the bottom of the tank, maintaining his speed and momentum, and came out of that water like a building launched from below and took the proffered fish daintily, like a girl accepting a mint. Then the whale fell back down in a long arc. His shadow blocked the sun for a moment and when he hit the surface of the aquarium it was as if a tree had toppled into the sea from a high ridge.

Then a massive wave, in answer, broke over the railing and drenched the crowd with seawater from row one to row twenty-three. You watched Dreadnought do his act and bathed at the same time, the salt water running out of your hair, smelling of the essence of whale.

As he made the circuit around his pool again, urging himself toward his moment of piebald beauty in the Florida sun, lifting out toward the heavy-scented odors of citrus and bougainvillea, we could glimpse his white-bottomed streaking image in the water and the amazing iridescences on his black head; he was the color of a good pair of saddle shoes. His dorsal fin was set like a black pyramid on his back and moved through the water like a blade hissing through nylon. His lines were clean and supple; his teeth were set in his grim mouth, each one the size of a table lamp. I had never seen such contained and implied power. Dreadnought leapt again and rang a bell that was suspended over the water. He opened his mouth and let the blond boy brush the whale's teeth with a janitor's broom. For his finale, Dreadnought came blasting out of the water, his flukes gleaming and shedding gallons of seawater, and the whale grasped a rope with his teeth and ran our American flag to the top of a flagpole high above the aquarium. Whenever the whale reached the apogee of one of his agile leaps, the crowd cheered, then braced itself for his graceful, streamlined plunge back into the water, when again we would be covered by a prodigious wave.

"Now that's an animal," Luke said.

"Can you imagine being hunted by a killer whale?" Savannah said.

Luke said to her, "If that thing's after you, Savannah, there's only one thing you can do. Submit. You'd have to submit to your fate."

"I'd love to see a whale like that in Colleton," I said, laughing.

"This is how they should execute criminals," Luke said suddenly. "Give them a bathing suit, stick a few mackerel in their jockstraps, and let them try to swim across this pool. If they made it they would go free. If they didn't, they'd really cut down on the food bill at Seaquarium.

"Real humane, Luke," said Savannah.

"I mean the really mean criminals. You know, the mass murderers. Hitler. Baby killers. The real creeps on the planet. I don't mean jaywalkers and shit."

"What a hideous death," I said, watching the whale leap through a ring of fire and douse the flames with the backwash of his landing.

"Naw, they could make it part of the act. Get Dad to run it. The killer whale jumps up and rings the bell, so as a reward, he gets to eat a criminal."

Dreadnought's last colossal free fall covered us with a final wave and we joined the hundreds of drenched tourists moving out toward the porpoise house.

After the killer whale, the porpoises looked diminutive and inconsequential and their act, though far more spunky and accomplished than the whale's, seemed trifling after Dreadnought's pièce de résistance. Their tricks were dazzlers, all right, they just weren't whales. But they were sure a happy, supererogatory tribe as they left the water like artillery shells leaping twenty feet in the air, their bodies jade-colored and smooth. Their heads were creased with perpetual harlequin smiles that lent sincerity to their high-spirited performances. They played baseball games, bowled, danced on their tails the full length of their aquarium, threw balls through hoops, and took lit cigarettes out of their trainer's mouth in a vain attempt to get him to give up smoking.

We found Carolina Snow in her own small enclosed pool, cut off from the companionship of the other porpoises. A large and curious crowd surrounded her enclosure and she swam from side to side, looking disoriented and faintly bored. She had not yet learned a single trick but was certainly earning her keep as an item of curiosity. The announcer described the capture of the white porpoise and made it sound like the most dangerous, exotic venture since the discovery of the Northwest Passage. At three o'clock we watched a keeper bring a bucket of fish to feed the Snow. He threw a blue runner at the opposite end of the pool from where Snow was swimming. She turned and in a movement of surprising delicacy accelerated across the pool and took the fish from the top of the water. We listened as the tourists tried to describe her color. We, her liberators, listened with pride as we heard strangers speak of her pale luminous beauty.

We watched the feeding and noticed that the man kept alternating where he threw the fish and that it was all part of an elaborate design for the training of the Snow. Once he got her in one rhythm of going from side to side in the pool, he reversed the procedure and brought her closer and closer until she lifted out of the water and took the last fish from his hand. The keeper was patient and skillful and the crowd applauded when Snow came out of the water. It was like watching a priest administering the Eucharist to a young girl in a Communion veil when he put the blue runner in Snow's open mouth.

"We got to get to a fish market, Tom," Luke whispered. "Savannah, you try to make contact with the night watchman before closing time. It don't close until eight."

"I've always wanted to play the wicked seductress," she said.

"You aren't seducing anyone. You're just going to make friends with him. Then put the son of a bitch to sleep."

In Coconut Grove we bought half a dozen whitings and a bucket of Kentucky Fried Chicken. When we returned to the Seaquarium it was a half-hour before closing time and we found Savannah talking with the night watchman, who had just arrived at the security office for duty.

"Brothers," Savannah said, "I have met the nicest man."

"Is she bothering you, mister?" Luke said. "She's only free

on a daily pass from the nut house."

"Bothering me? It's not often I get to talk to such a pretty girl. I'm the one who's usually here when everybody's gone home."

"Mr. Beavers is from New York City."

"You want some fried chicken?" Luke offered.

"Don't mind if I do," Mr. Beavers said, pulling out a drumstick.

"How about a Pepsi?"

"I'm strictly a coffee man. Hey, it's getting close to closing time. I got to run you kids out of here. This job gets lonely. That's its only drawback."

He sounded a loud foghorn that was followed immediately by a recorded announcement asking that all visitors leave the grounds of the Seaquarium at once and giving the opening time for the next day. Mr. Beavers went outside his office door and blew his own whistle, walking between the killer whale amphitheater and the porpoise house. Savannah refreshed his coffee from the pot he had already brewed on his desk, snapped open the contents of two sleeping pills, and stirred the coffee until the powder dissolved completely.

Luke and I followed Mr. Beavers around the park as he good-humoredly urged the tourists to go home and return the next day. He stopped at the holding tank where the Snow was moving restlessly from one side to the other.

"She's an aberration of nature," he said. "But a beautiful aberration."

As he turned, he spotted a teenager throwing a Popsicle wrapper on the ground. "My good young man," he said, "littering is a crime against the maker of this green earth."

As he walked toward the boy, Luke dropped the whiting into the water of Carolina Snow's aquarium. The Snow passed it twice before she downed it.

"How many pills did you put in that fish?" I whispered.

"Enough to kill you or me," he answered.

Mr. Beavers was sipping his coffee as we waved goodbye to

him. I whispered to Savannah as we walked to the pickup, "Nice work, Mata Hari."

Luke came walking up behind us and said, "I'm hot. How 'bout let's go swimming in Key Biscayne."

"What time are we coming back for the Snow," I asked.

"I figure about midnight," he said.

We watched the moon rise like a pale watermark against the eastern sky. We swam until the sun began to set in an Atlantic so different from the ocean that broke against our part of the eastern seaboard that it did not seem possible that they were related in any way. The Florida ocean was clear-eyed and aquarmarine and I had never been able to see my own feet as I walked chest-deep in the sea.

"This water don't seem right," Luke said, expressing exactly what I felt.

The sea has always been feminine to me but Florida had softened its hard edges and tamed the azury depths with clarity. The mystery of Florida deepened on the shore as we ate mangoes for the first time. The fruit tasted foreign but indigenous, like sunlight a tree had changed through patience. We were strangers to a sea you could trust, whose tides were imperceptible and gentle, whose cologne-colored waters were translucent and calm below the palm trees. The moon laid a filament of silver across the water for a hundred miles before it nested in the braids of Savannah's hair. Luke stood up and fished his watch out from his jeans pocket.

"If we get caught tonight, Tom and Savannah, just let me do the talking. I got you into this and it's my responsibility to get you out if we hit trouble. Now let's pray that Mr. Beavers is counting sheep."

Through the window of his small office we could see Mr. Beavers with his head on his desk, sleeping soundly. Luke backed the pickup into a grove of trees by the Cyclone fence and, working quickly, cut a large hole in the fence using his wire cutters. Entering the fence, we made our way through the shadows passing over the moat of sharks where we could hear the creatures moving through the water below us in their end-less circuit, their horrible punishment for having been born sharks. We were running by the amphitheater when we heard the sound of the killer whale's implosion of breath.

"Wait a minute," Luke said, removing a fish from the bag he had brought for Snow in case she wanted a snack on the ride north.

"No Luke," I said, alarmed. "We don't have time for no foolishness."

But Luke was running up the stairs into the amphitheater and Savannah and I had no choice but to follow him. In the moonlight we watched him as he climbed the platform and we saw the great fin break the water below him. Then Luke moved to the edge of the platform, and mimicking the gestures of the blond trainer we had witnessed earlier in the day, he made a circular movement with his arm and we saw Dread-nought dive deep into his tank and heard the punished waters slapping against the sides of the aquarium as the invisible whale gathered speed beneath my brother. Luke put the whit-ing in his right hand and leaned far out over the water.

The whale exploded out from below and took the whiting from Luke's hand without so much as grazing his fingers. Then the lordly fall from space carried the whale over on his side, exposing his brilliant white underbelly, and he washed twenty-three rows of bleachers as he entered the water again in a fabulous wave.

"Stupid, stupid, stupid," I whispered as Luke joined us again.

"Wonderful, wonderful, wonderful," Savannah said, ex-hilarated.

We ran to *The Amberjack* and went to the storage bin on deck where the crew kept the equipment we knew we would need. Luke pulled out the ropes and the stretcher. He threw the foam rubber mattresses to Savannah. She took them and raced back to the truck to lay them out neatly on the flatbed. Luke and I hurried to the porpoise house and Luke again used his wire cutters to enter the area where the Snow was kept.

We reached her just in time. She was almost motionless in shallow water and I think she would have drowned if we had waited another hour. When we entered the water, she was so drugged that she did not even move. We caught her beneath the head and stomach and moved her over to the side of the pool where we had placed the stretcher. She was so white my hand looked brown against her head. She made a tender, human sound as we floated her across the pool. Savanna returned and the three of us girded the stretcher beneath her in the water and bound her with the ropes in three places.

Again, we passed through the shadows of palms and citrus trees, Luke and I bearing the stretcher like medics in a war zone, keeping low and moving fast. We passed through the opening in the ruined fence and untied the Snow gently and rolled her onto the mattresses. Savannah and I splashed her with the Key Biscayne water we had gathered in buckets and in our beer cooler. Luke closed the tailgate, and running to the cab, he started the motor and eased out of the parking lot and moved down the causeway toward the lights of Miami. I think we were the nearest to getting caught in those first two minutes, because going down that nearly deserted highway, the three Wingo kids from South Carolina were screaming, screaming, screaming.

Soon we had left Miami forever and Luke had his foot pressed against the accelerator almost to the floorboard, and the warm air streamed through our hair as every mile brought us closer to the border of Georgia. Snow's breathing was ragged at first, like the tearing of paper, and once or twice when it seemed as though she had stopped breathing I blew air into her blowhole. She answered me with a breath of her own but the effect of the pills did not seem to wear off until we stopped for gas at Daytona Beach. Then she rallied and was perky for the rest of the trip.

After we got gas, Luke drove the truck out onto the beach and Savannah and I leapt out and filled up the buckets and cooler with fresh seawater, then hopped back in as Luke spun through the sand and made it to the highway again. "We're doing it. We're doing it," he screamed out the back window to us. "We got five more hours and we'll be home free."

We doused the porpoise with salt water and massaged her from head to tail to keep her circulation going and spoke to her with those phrases of endearment kids normally reserve for dogs. She was supple and pliable and her flesh was satiny to the touch. We sang lullabies to her, recited children's poems and nursery rhymes, and whispered that we were taking her home and she would never have to eat dead fish again. When we crossed into Georgia, Savannah and I danced around the flatbed and Luke had to slow down because he thought we might dance ourselves right out of the truck.

It was right outside of Midway, Georgia, that a highway patrolman pulled Luke over for going about forty miles over the speed limit. Luke said through the back wind, "Cover Snow's head with one of those mattresses. I'll handle this."

The sun had already risen and the patrolman was young and slim as a blade. He had that maddening arrogance of the rookie. But Luke bounded out of that truck just bubbling over about something.

"Officer," I heard him say as Savannah and I got Snow's head covered. "I'm so sorry. Honest I am. But I was so excited about catching this here shark and I just had to get it back so my daddy could see it while it was still alive."

The patrolman came over to the truck and whistled as he looked in.

"He's a big'un," the patrolman said. "But that's no cause for you speeding like that, son."

"You don't understand, Officer," Luke said. "This here is a world record. I caught him with a rod and reel. It's a white shark. They're the real man-eaters. I caught this one near the jetty off Saint Simons Island."

"What'd you catch him with?"

"I caught him with a live shrimp, if you can believe such a thing. They caught a white shark in Florida last year and found a man's boot and shinbone in his stomach."

"I got to give you a ticket, son."

"I expect that, sir. I was speeding I was so excited. You ever catch a fish this big?"

"I'm from Marietta. I once caught a twelve-pound bass in Lake Lanier."

"Then you know exactly how I feel, sir. Look, let me show you his teeth. He's got teeth like razor blades. My poor brother and sister are half dead from trying to hold this rascal down. Let the officer have a look, Tom."

"I don't cotton to seeing no shark, son. Just you run along now and slow it down a bit. I guess you got a right to be excited. That bass I caught, that was the biggest one taken out of Lake Lanier that whole day. My cat ate it before I could show it to my daddy."

"Thank you so much, sir. You sure you don't want to see its teeth? He's got a powerful mouthful."

"I'd sure rather be driving than sitting on that dang thing," the patrolman said to me and Savannah as he walked back to his car.

My mother was hanging out wash when we came blitzing down the dirt road and Luke made a few triumphant doughnuts on the lawn and we slid to a stop. My mother ran to the truck and did a little softshoe of triumph around the lawn, her arms raised in the air. Luke backed up the truck to the sea wall and we rolled the porpoise back onto the stretcher. Mama kicked off her shoes and the four of us stepped into the high tide and moved out toward deeper water. We held Snow in our arms and walked her into deeper water, letting her get used to the river again. We let her float by herself but she seemed unbalanced and unsure of herself. Luke held her head above the water until I felt her powerful tail flip me off her and she began to swim slowly and unsteadily away from us. For fifteen minutes she looked like a dying animal and it was painful to watch her suffer. We stood on the dock praying for her, my mother leading us through a rosary without beads. The Snow floundered; she seemed to have trouble breathing; her sense of balance and timing were not functioning. Then it changed before our eyes. Instinct returned and she dove and the old sense of rhythm and grace returned in the easy fluency of that dive. She sounded after a long minute and was two hundred yards further out in the river.

"She's made it," Luke yelled, and we gathered together, holding on to each other. I was exhausted, sweaty, famished, but I had never felt so wonderful in my life.

Up she rose again and, turning, she passed us standing on the dock.

We cheered and screamed and wept. And we danced a new dance on our floating dock on the most beautiful island in the world on the finest, the very finest, day of Tom Wingo's life.

Vocabulary

We can learn a lot about what a word means by examining the surrounding context. The following words are used to describe the white dolphin in the first paragraph on page 183.

luxurious

silken

promenade

silvered

sublimity

vulnerability

ambient

chevron

apotheosis

imperceptibly

lunar

alchemy

argentine

a. How many do you know already without consulting the dictionary? Read the list and guess what they could mean.

b. After you have made your guess, locate the following words in the text and read the paragraph. Again guess what the words mean.

c. Now confirm/correct your guess by looking each word up in the dictionary.

d. How many of the definitions became clear once you read the paragraph?

Group Activities

A. In Groups: Visualize the concrete images. Which scenes came to life as you were reading? Share the notations you made with the other members of your group. Decide on one scene to draw. Everyone in your group can participate in drawing the scene. Try to make it as accurate and as detailed as possible so that it will be readily identifiable.

After you finish the drawings hold them up for the entire class to see. Have your classmates:

try to identify the scene

find the line(s) in the chapter that the drawing depicts

Swap drawings with another group and see if you can find details that were left out of the drawing.

B. Mrs. Wingo learns that her children are responsible for the successful return of Carolina Snow to her home. She becomes extremely angry when she considers the risk and danger involved; she would have also been humiliated had they been caught and arrested. She confronts one of the children about their involvement; in groups of three or four peers, brainstorm and create that conversation between Mrs. Wingo and either Tom, Luke or Savannah.

Extra Credit—Writing Fiction

Author Pat Conroy's passionate account of the hunt, capture and rescue of the white dolphin, Carolina Snow, is a fine example of eloquent and captivating storytelling. If you have ever wanted to write short stories or a novel, complete the following exercises using Conroy's plot and characters as examples.

Plot Development

According to Oakly Hall, author of *The Art and Craft of Novel Writing*, (*Writers Digest Books*) we can define a story as "a narrative of events arranged in their time-sequence." He says "a plot is a story plus causal relationships in a meaningful sequence." Good fiction is defined as "strong plots founded on strong characters."

Would you say that Pat Conroy developed a strong plot founded on strong characters?

Character Development

Complete a Character Analysis Worksheet for:

Henry—father of Tom, Luke and Savannah

Luke—his son

What character traits do they have in common? What traits are different? Imagine they have both applied for a job with your company. They have the same skill level. Which one would you hire?

The Development of Action in Fiction

Author Pat Conroy created an imaginative, thorough, and believable plan for the rescue of Carolina Snow. Before writing this scene he probably researched and outlined in detail all the action. As he began to write, he could use his plan as a reference point to assure the scene would be complete, understandable, and in appropriate time sequence.

Try to imagine what Conroy's outline included. Reread the rescue scenes and develop a similar outline, begin with Luke, Savannah, and Tom's arrival at the Miami Seaquarium. On the left hand side of the paper write the time the action is to take place. On the right side, write the desired action. Conroy's final text will give you all the data you need.

Example

11:00 a.m.	Visit Seaquarium
	Inspect grounds and observe guard house
	Locate *Amberjack*
12:00 p.m.	Watch killer whale show/dolphin show
3:00 p.m.	Observe feeding of Carolina Snow in order to replicate later with drugged fish.

Developing an action plan or plot

Based on Conroy's storyline, write at least two objectives for each goal of the following characters.

The goal of Tom, Luke and Savannah was: Free Carolina Snow and return her to the sea as soon as possible.

The crew of the Amberjack's goal: Capture the white porpoise of Colleton alive.

The townspeople of Colleton's goal: Keep the crew of the Amberjack from capturing the porpoise.

Writing Assignment—The Short Story

Review your goals and objectives on pages 189 and 190 in *Career Choices* and your Character Analysis Worksheet on page 27. Develop a fictional character based on your chart. Choose one or two of your goals and write a short story paying close attention to character development and sequential, meaningful action.

Attention future novelists, storytellers and recreational writers! If you really enjoy storytelling and writing fiction, take a look at your completed assignment on page 223 of *Career Choices*; the 10 year workplan for the immigrant, Yorik. You may have the beginnings of a novel.

Pat Conroy 1945–

Pat Conroy, a native of the southern United States, is a 1967 graduate of Citadel. *The Prince of Tides*, first published in 1986, was one of that year's best-selling novels. His other titles include; *The Water is Wide, The Great Santini,* and *The Lords of Discipline.* He lives in Atlanta, Georgia, with his wife and four children.

Journal entry:
> Have you ever had a dream that you gave up on? Why
> did you abandon it? Was it for a good reason? Have you
> thought about the dream since? How do you feel about
> it now?

A Dream Deferred

by Langston Hughes

Harlem

What happens to a dream deferred?

Does it dry up
like a raisin in the sun?
Or fester like a sore—
And then run?
Does it stink like rotten meat?
Or crust and sugar over—
like a syrup—sweet?

Maybe it just sags
like a heavy load.

Or does it explode?

1. What is the opening question? How does the final line respond to that question?

2. List the similes that you find in the poem.

3. How does each simile suggest a different attitude that people might take in response to delaying achievement?

4. In what ways might this poem be dealing with the theme of equality?

5. Read Martin Luther King's speech, "I Have a Dream . . ." on page 27. How does King's discussion of his dream relate to Hughes' image of the deferred dream?

6. Is there a dream you are thinking of giving up? Write the dream at the top of a piece of paper. Then draw a line down the middle of the page. On the left side of the paper, list all of the reasons why you should give it up. On the right side, list all of the reasons why you should stick with it. Re-read and analyze your findings. Carry this paper with you for a week or two and read it daily. Don't give up on your dream unless it is absolutely necessary or until it no longer appeals to you.

   Optional: Form a group with three or four classmates. Share your lists and then brainstorm ways you can over-come the obstacles that are keeping you from your dream.

7. Complete the activity on page 215 of *Career Choices*.

Journal entry:
> Have you ever wanted to give up on a dream or seeking the life you wanted because you thought that life was unfair? Perhaps you have a handicap, grew up in poverty, made a poor choice that hurt you in some way. Maybe you don't feel like you are in the mainstream of society.
>
> Read and discuss pages 194 and 195 in *Career Choices*.

Mother to Son

by Langston Hughes

Well, son, I'll tell you:
Life for me ain't been no crystal stair.
It's had tacks in it,
And splinters,
And boards torn up,
And places with no carpet on the floor—
Bare.
But all the time
I'se been a-climbin' on,
And reachin' landin's,
And turnin' corners,
And sometimes goin' in the dark
Where there ain't been no light.
So, boy, don't you turn back.
Don't you set down on the steps
'Cause you finds it's kinder hard.
Don't you fall now—

For I'se still goin', honey,
I'se still climbin',
And life for me ain't been no crystal stair.

---

1. Who is the speaker in this poem?
2. What is the situation?
3. What advice does the mother give to her son?
4. What image does a "crystal stair" evoke?
5. How does the mother describe the circumstances of her life?
6. Despite the obstacles, what is the mother encouraging the child to do?
7. How is this mother a positive role model for her son?
8. Why do you think that some people persist and often succeed despite all odds?
9. What advice do your loved ones give to you?
10. Can you think of friends or a member of your family who have pushed on when all odds were against them? Interview one of them and then share their story in an essay or as a presentation to the class.

A Noiseless Patient Spider

by Walt Whitman

A noiseless patient spider,
I mark'd where on a little promontory it stood isolated,
Mark'd how to explore the vacant vast surrounding,
It launch'd forth filament, filament, filament, out of itself,
Ever unreeling them, ever tirelessly speeding them,
And you O my soul, where you stand,
Surrounded, detached, in measureless oceans of space,
Ceaselessly musing, venturing, throwing, seeking the
    spheres to connect them,
Till the bridge you will need be form'd, till the ductile
    anchor hold,
Till the gossamer thread you fling catch somewhere,
    O my soul.

What is the central metaphor in this poem? Explain how this comparison conveys the theme of the poem.

If the spider stands for a soul, and the spider is trying to complete a web, what is the soul attempting to do?

excerpt from
All I Really Need to Know I learned in Kindergarten

by Robert Fulghum

This is my neighbor. Nice lady. Coming out her front door, on her way to work and in her "looking good" mode. She's locking the door now and picking up her daily luggage: purse, lunch bag, gym bag for aerobics, and the garbage bucket to take out. She turns, sees me, gives me the big, smiling Hello, takes three steps across her front porch. And goes "AAAAAAAAGGGGGGGGGHHHHHHHHHHH!!!!" *(That's a direct quote.)* At about the level of a fire engine at full cry. Spider web! She has walked full force into a spider web. And the pressing question, of course: Just where is the spider *now?*

She flings her baggage in all directions. And at the same time does a high-kick, jitterbug sort of dance—like a mating stork in crazed heat. Clutches at her face and hair and goes "AAAAAAAGGGGGGGGHHHHHHHHHH!!!!!" at a new level of intensity. Tries opening the front door without unlocking it. Tries again. Breaks key in the lock. Runs around the house headed for the back door. Doppler effect of

"AAAAAGGGHHHHaaggh . . ."

Now a different view of this scene. Here is the spider. Rather ordinary, medium gray, middle-aged lady spider. She's been up since before dawn working on her web, and all is well. Nice day, no wind, dew point just right to keep things sticky. She's out checking the moorings and thinking about the little gnats she'd like to have for breakfast. Feeling good. Ready for action. All of a sudden all hell breaks loose—earthquake, tornado, volcano. The web is torn loose and is wrapped around a frenzied moving haystack, and a huge piece of raw-but-painted meat is making a sound the spider never heard before: "AAAAAAAGGGGGGGGHHHHHHHHHH!!!!!!" It's too big to wrap up and eat later, and it's moving too much to hold down. Jump for it? Hang on and hope? Dig in?

Human being. She has caught a human being. And the pressing question is, of course: Where is it going and what will it do when it gets there?

The neighbor lady thinks the spider is about the size of a lobster and has big rubber lips and poisonous fangs. The neighbor lady will probably strip to the skin and take a full shower and shampoo just to make sure it's gone—and then put on a whole new outfit to make certain she is not inhabited.

The spider? Well, if she survives all this, she will really

have something to talk about—the one that got away that was THIS BIG. "And you should have seen the JAWS on the thing!"

Spiders. Amazing creatures. Been around maybe 350 million years, so they can cope with about anything. Lots of them, too—sixty or seventy thousand per suburban acre. It's the web thing that I envy. Imagine what it would be like if people were equipped like spiders. If we had this little six-nozzled aperture right at the base of our spine and we could make yards of something like glass fiber with it. Wrapping packages would be a cinch! Mountain climbing would never be the same. Think of the Olympic events. And mating and child rearing would take on new dimensions. Well, you take it from there. It boggles the mind. Cleaning up human-sized webs would be a mess, on the other hand.

All this reminds me of a song I know. And you know, too. And your parents and your children, they know. About the eensy-weensy spider. Went up the waterspout. Down came the rain and washed the spider out. Out came the sun and dried up all the rain. And the eensy-weensy spider went up the spout again. You probably know the motions, too.

What's the deal here? Why do we all know that song? Why do we keep passing it on to our kids? Especially when it puts spiders in such a favorable light? Nobody goes "AAAAAAAGGGGGGGGHHHHHHHH!!!!!" when they sing it. Maybe because it puts the life adventure in such clear and simple terms. The small creature is alive and looks for adventure. Here's the drainpipe—a long tunnel going up toward some light. The spider doesn't even think about it—just goes. Disaster befalls it—rain, flood, powerful forces. And the spider is knocked down and out beyond where it started. Does the spider say, "To hell with that"? No. Sun comes out—clears things up—dries off the spider. And the small creature goes over to the drainpipe and looks up and thinks it *really* wants to know what is up there. It's a little wiser now—checks the sky first, looks for better toeholds, says a spider prayer, and heads up through mystery toward the light and wherever.

Living things have been doing just that for a long, long time. Through every kind of disaster and setback and catastrophe. We are survivors. And we teach our kids about that. And maybe spiders tell their kids about it, too, in their spider sort of way.

So the neighbor lady will survive and be a little wiser coming out the door on her way to work. And the spider, if it lives, will do likewise. And if not, well, there are lots more spiders, and the word gets around. Especially when the word is "AAAAAAAGGGGGGGGHHHHHHHHH!!!!"

---

1. Why does Fulghum use a common spider to convey his message?

2. What is his message?

3. What is noteworthy about the spider? What could we learn from the spider's persistent efforts?

4. Compare the analogy used by Fulghum in this excerpt to the spider metaphor used in Walt Whitman's poem.

5. "The Itsy Bitsy Spider" was a song most of us learned in Kindergarten. Can you think of a story you heard as a child that also encouraged readers to: "keep going; don't give up; if at first you don't succeed, try, try again"?

6. How would you describe Fulghum's style of writing? How is it different from Emerson's ("Self-Reliance") style?

7. A creed is a statement of beliefs, principals, or opinions. It usually starts with the phrase "I believe." Taped over Fulghum's desk is the following storyteller's creed.

> I believe that imagination is stronger than knowledge.
>
> That myth is more potent than history.
>
> That dreams are more powerful than facts.
>
> That hope always triumphs over experience.
>
> That laughter is the only cure for grief.
>
> And I believe that love is stronger than death.

Before you read Fulghum's biography try to imagine his personality. What does this creed say about the values of this man? Once you read his biography, what else can you imagine about him. Would he make a good research scientist, accountant or surgeon? Why or why not?

8. Write the creed you would tape over your desk.

Robert Fulghum 1937–

Robert Fulghum considers himself a philosopher. He likes to think a lot about ordinary things and then express himself by writing, speaking or painting. In his lifetime, he has been a working cowboy, a folksinger, an IBM salesman, an artist, a minister, a bartender, and an art teacher. He is a father and lives with his wife on a houseboat in Seattle.

Journal entry:
> Have you ever thought about the lifestyle that you would like to have when you retire? Do your parents/guardians have a retirement account? Ask them about their plans for retirement. Do you know any people who are beyond working age? What is their lifestyle like?

Over the Hill to the Poor-house

by Will M. Carleton

Over the hill to the poor-house I'm trudgin' my weary way—
I, a woman of seventy, and only a trifle gray—
I, who am smart an' chipper, for all the years I've told,
As many another woman that's only half as old.

Over the hill to the poor-house—I can't quite make it clear!
Over the hill to the poor-house—and it seems so horrid queer!
Many a step I've taken a-toiln' to and fro,
But this is a sort of journey I never thought to go.

What is the use of heapin' on me a pauper's shame?
Am I lazy or crazy? am I blind or lame?
True, I am not so supple, nor yet so awful stout;
But charity ain't' no favor, if one can live without.

I am willin' and anxious an' ready any day
To work for a decent livin', an' pay my honest way;
For I can earn my victuals an' more too, I'll be bound,
If anybody only is willin' to have me round.

Continued

Once I was young an' han'some—I was, upon my soul—
Once my cheeks was roses, my eyes as black as coal;
And I can't remember, in them days, of hearin' people say,
For any kind of a reason, that I was in their way.

'T ain't no use of boastin', or talkin' over free,
But many a house an' home was open then to me;
Many a han'some offer I had from likely men,
And nobody ever hinted that I was a burden then.

And when to John I was married, sure he was good and smart,
But he and all the neighbors would own I done my part;
For life was all before me, an' I was young an' strong,
And I worked the best that I could in tryin' to get along.

And so we worked together: and life was hard, but gay,
With now and then a baby for to cheer us on our way;
Till we had half a dozen, an' all growed clean an' neat,
An' went to school like others, an' had enough to eat.

So we worked for the child'rn, and raised 'em every one;
Worked for 'em summer and winter, just as we ought to 've done;
Only perhaps we humored 'em, which some good folks condemn,
But every couple's child'rn's a heap the best to them.

Strange how much we think of our blessed little ones!—
I'd have died for my daughters, I'd have died for my sons!
And God he made that rule of love; but when we're old and gray,
I've noticed it sometimes somehow fails to work the other way.

Strange, another thing: when our boys an' girls was grown,
And when, exceptin' Charley, they'd left us there alone,
When John he nearer an' nearer come, an' dearer seemed to be,
The Lord of Hosts he come one day an' took him away from me.

Still I was bound to struggle, an' never to cringe or fall—
Still I worked for Charley, for Charley was now my all;
And Charley was pretty good to me, with scarce a word or frown,
Till at last he went a-courtin', and brought a wife from town.

She was somewhat dressy, an' hadn't a pleasant smile—
She was quite conceity, and carried a heap o' style;
But if ever I tried to be friends, I did with her, I know;
But she was hard and proud, an' I couldn't make it go.

She had an edication, an' that was good for her;
But when she twitted me on mine, 't was carryin' things too fur;
An' I told her once, 'fore company (an' it almost made her sick),
That I never swallowed a grammar, or 'et a 'rithmetic.

So 't was only a few days before the thing was done—
They was a family of themselves, and I another one;
And a very little cottage one family will do,
But I never have seen a house that was big enough for two.

An' I never could speak to suit her, never could please her eye,
An' it made me independent, an' then I didn't try;
But I was terribly staggered, an' felt it like a blow,
When Charley turned ag'in me, an' told me I could go.

I went to live with Susan, but Susan's house was small,
And she was always a-hintin' how snug it was for us all;
And what with her husband's sisters, and what with child'rn three,
'T was easy to discover that there wasn't room for me.

An' then I went to Thomas, the oldest son I've got,
For Thomas' buildings'd cover the half of an acre lot;
But all the child'rn was on me—I couldn't stand their sauce—
And Thomas said I needn't think I was comin' there to boss.

An' then I wrote to Rebecca, my girl who lives out West,
And to Isaac, not far from her—some twenty miles at best;
And one of 'em said 't was too warm there for anyone so old,
And t'other had an opinion the climate was too cold.

So they have shirked and slighted me, an' shifted me about—
So they have well-nigh soured me, an' wore my old heart out;
But still I've born up pretty well, an' wasn't much put down,
Till Charley went to the poor-master, an' put me on the town.

Continued

Over the hill to the poor-house—my child'm dear, good-by!
Many a night I've watched you when only God was nigh;
And God'll judge between us; but I will al'ays pray
That you shall never suffer the half I do today.

---

1. Describe how you feel after reading the poem.

2. What do you think the author's purpose was for writing this poem?

3. Why do you think that this author wrote from a woman's point of view?

4. Do you think that the actions of the woman's children were justified? Would you treat your parents that way? Can you imagine your children treating you that way?

5. Are you aware of the statistics about poverty among the elderly? Visit your library and find out what percentage of people over the age of 65 live below the poverty line. What percentage are women? What percentage are men?

6. What can you do in the next fifty years to make sure that you won't be living in poverty when you are no longer able to work?

7. Complete the "Economics of Bad Habits" exercise on page 208 and 209 of *Career Choices*. Pay particular attention to the top of page 209. This demonstrates the effects of depositing money in a retirement account every month/year. Would the woman in this poem have been in this predicament had she followed this strategy?

Writing Assignment

Imagine that you are seventy years old. Describe your life. Where do you live. Who are the important people in your life? What are your hobbies? What do you do every day? Take the reader through a typical day in your life.

Journal entry:

Have you ever regretted a decision not to do something because you were afraid or felt anxious? Describe that situation and how you felt about it.

What is the definition of anxiety?

George Gray

by Edgra Lee Masters

I have studied many times
The marble which was chiseled for me—
A boat with a furled sail at rest in a harbor.
In truth it pictures not my destination
But my life.
For love was offered me and I shrank from its disillusionment;
Sorrow knocked at my door, but I was afraid;
Ambition called to me, but I dreaded the chances.
Yet all the while I hungered for meaning in my life.
And now I know that we must lift the sail
And catch the winds of destiny
Wherever they drive the boat.
To put meaning in one's life may end in madness,
But life without meaning is the torture
Of restlessness and vague desire—
It is a boat longing for the sea and yet afraid.

1. What kind of a man is described here?

2. How is the use of the name "Gray" symbolic?

3. What are George's regrets?

4. Choose one of the following lines from the poem and use your imagination to create a portion of George Gray's life story. What do you think happened? You may want to draw upon a story you heard from a friend or family member.

   > For love was offered me and I shrank from its disillusionment;
   >
   > Sorrow knocked at my door, but I was afraid
   >
   > Ambition called to me, but I dreaded the chances.

   How can you avoid having similar regrets at the end of your life? Review pages 216 to 221 in **Career Choices**.

Edgra Lee Masters 1869–1950

Edgra Lee Masters was born in Kansas and raised in two small towns in Illinois. His family moved to Lewistown, Illinois, and he studied law there with his father. He set up a legal practice of his own in Chicago and from 1892-1901 he wrote and published pamphlets on political issues. Masters' interest in law and politics was matched by an interest in poetry. *Spoon River Anthology* and *The New Spoon River* are among his most widely read collections. Masters stated that Lewistown furnished him with "a key which unlocked the secrets of the world at large" in his creation of *Spoon River Anthology*. This book is a collection of monologues by various characters, all of them dead, who reflect honestly and with intense feeling about their lives. His acid commentaries attacked the sterile small town life "indigenous to Midwestern soil." Lawyers, editors, bankers, and superintendents were among those who were portrayed negatively. "George Gray" illustrates Masters' ability to condense the regrets of an entire life in a brief, but powerful speech.

Journal entry:
> Imagine that you have been wanting to be invited to a
> party to be hosted by a classmate. You get invited and of
> course you accept. Later that day you hear some friends
> talking about the clothes they are going to wear; expen-
> sive jeans, the "right" brand of tennis shoes etc. Your
> family has only been able to buy the brands sold at large
> chain discount stores. What would you do?

The Necklace

by Guy De Maupassant

She was one of those pretty and charming girls who, by
some freak of destiny, are born into families that have always
held subordinate appointments. Possessing neither dowry nor
expectations, she had no hope of meeting some man of wealth
and distinction, who would understand her, fall in love with
her, and wed her. So she consented to marry a small clerk in
the Ministry of Public Instruction.

She dressed plainly, because she could not afford to be
elegant, but she felt as unhappy as if she had married beneath
her. Women are dependent on neither caste nor ancestry.
With them, beauty, grace, and charm take the place of birth
and breeding. In their case, natural delicacy, instinctive refinement, and adaptability constitute their claims to aristocracy
and raise girls of the lower classes to an equality with the
greatest of great ladies. She was eternally restive under the
conviction that she had been born to enjoy every refinement
and luxury. Depressed by her humble surroundings, the sordid
walls of her dwelling, its worn furniture and shabby fabrics

were a torment to her. Details which another woman of her class would scarcely have noticed, tortured her and filled her with resentment. The sight of her little Breton maid-of-all-work roused in her forlorn repinings and frantic yearnings. She pictured to herself silent antechambers, upholstered with oriental tapestry, lighted by great bronze standard lamps, where two tall footmen in knee breeches slumbered in huge arm-chairs, overcome by the oppressive heat from the stove. She dreamed of spacious drawing-rooms with hangings of antique silk, and beautiful tables laden with priceless ornaments: of fragrant and coquettish boudoirs, exquisitely adapted for afternoon chats with intimate friends, men of note and distinction, whose attentions are coveted by every woman.

She would sit down to dinner at the round table, its cloth already three days old, while her husband, seated opposite to her, removed the lid from the soup tureen and exclaimed, 'Pot-au-feu! How splendid! My favourite soup!' But her own thoughts were dallying with the idea of exquisite dinners and shining silver, in rooms whose tapestried walls were gay with antique figures and grotesque birds in fairy forests. She would dream of delicious dishes served on wonderful plate, of soft, whispered nothings, which evoke a sphinx-like smile, while one trifles with the pink flesh of a trout or the wing of a plump pullet.

She had no pretty gowns, no jewels, nothing—and yet she cared for nothing else. She felt that it was for such things as these that she had been born. What joy it would have given her to attract, to charm, to be envied by women, courted by men! She had a wealthy friend, who had been at school at the same convent, but after a time she refused to go and see her, because she suffered so acutely after each visit. She spent whole days in tears of grief, regret, despair, and misery.

One evening her husband returned home in triumph with a large envelope in his hand.

'Here is something for you,' he cried.

Hastily she tore open the envelope and drew out a printed

card with the following inscription:

'The Minister of Public Instruction and Madame Georges Ramponneau have the honour to request the company of Monsieur and Madame Loisel at an At Home at the Education Office on Monday, 18th January.'

Instead of being delighted as her husband had hoped, she flung the invitation irritably on the table, exclaiming:

'What good is that to me?'

'Why, my dear, I thought you would be pleased. You never go anywhere, and this is a really splendid chance for you. I had no end of trouble in getting it. Everybody is trying to get an invitation. It's very select, and only a few invitations are issued to the clerks. You will see all the officials there.'

She looked at him in exasperation, and exclaimed petulantly:

'What do you expect me to wear at a reception like that?'

He had not considered the matter, but he replied hesitatingly:

'What, that dress you always wear to the theatre seems to me very nice indeed. . .'

He broke off. To his horror and consternation he saw that his wife was in tears. Two large drops were rolling slowly down her cheeks.

'What on earth is the matter?' he gasped.

With a violent effort she controlled her emotion, and drying her wet cheeks said in a calm voice:

'Nothing. Only I haven't a frock, and so I can't go to the reception. Give your invitation to some friend in your office, whose wife is better dressed than I am.'

He was greatly distressed.

'Let us talk it over, Mathilde. How much do you think a proper frock would cost, something quite simple that would come in useful for other occasions afterwards?'

She considered the matter for a few moments, busy with her calculations, and wondering how large a sum she might venture to name without shocking the little clerk's instincts of economy and provoking a prompt refusal.

'I hardly know,' she said at last, doubtfully, 'But I think I could manage with four hundred francs.'

He turned a little pale. She had named the exact sum that he had saved for buying a gun and treating himself to some Sunday shooting parties the following summer with some friends, who were going to shoot larks in the plain of Nanterre. But he replied:

'Very well, I'll give you four hundred francs. But mind you buy a really handsome gown.'

     .   .   .   .   .

The day of the party drew near. But although her gown was finished, Madame Loisel seemed depressed and dissatisfied.

'What is the matter?' asked her husband one evening.

'You haven't been at all yourself the last three days.'

She answered: 'It vexes me to think that I haven't any jewellery to wear, not even a brooch. I shall feel like a perfect pauper. I would almost rather not go to the party.'

'You can wear some fresh flowers. They are very fashionable this year. For ten francs you can get two or three splendid roses.'

She was not convinced.

'No, there is nothing more humiliating than to have an air of poverty among a crowd of rich women.'

'How silly you are!' exclaimed her husband. 'Why don't you ask your friend, Madame Forestier, to lend you some jewellery. You know her quite well enough for that.'

She uttered a cry of joy.

'Yes, of course, it never occurred to me.'

The next day she paid her friend a visit and explained her predicament.

Madame Forestier went to her wardrobe, took out a large jewel case and placed it open before her friend.

'Help yourself, my dear,' she said.

Madame Loisel saw some bracelets, a pearl necklace, a Venetian cross exquisitely worked in gold and jewels. She tried on these ornaments in front of the mirror and hesitated, reluctant to take them off and give them back.

'Have you nothing else?' she kept asking.

'Oh yes, look for yourself. I don't know what you would prefer.'

At length, she discovered a black satin case containing a superb diamond necklace, and her heart began to beat with frantic desire. With trembling hands she took it out, fastened it over her high-necked gown, and stood gazing at herself in rapture.

Then, in an agony of doubt, she said:

'Will you lend me this? I shouldn't want anything else.'

'Yes, certainly.'

She threw her arms around her friend's neck, kissed her effusively, and then fled with her treasure.

.   .   .   .   .

It was the night of the reception. Madame Loisel's triumph was complete. All smiles and graciousness, in her exquisite gown, she was the prettiest woman in the room. Her head was a whirl of joy. All the men stared at her and inquired her name and begged for an introduction; all the junior staff asked her for waltzes. She even attracted the attention of the minister himself.

Carried away by her enjoyment, glorying in her beauty and her success, she threw herself ecstatically into the dance. She moved as in a beatific dream, wherein were mingled all the homage and admiration she had evoked, all the desires she had kindled, all that complete and perfect triumph, so dear to a woman's heart.

It was close on four before she could tear herself away. Ever since midnight her husband had been dozing in a little, deserted drawing-room together with three other men whose wives were enjoying themselves immensely.

He threw her outdoor wraps round her shoulders, unpretentious, every-day garments, whose shabbiness contrasted strangely with the elegance of her ball dress. Conscious of the incongruity, she was eager to be gone, in order to escape the notice of the other women in their luxurious furs. Loisel tried to restrain her.

'Wait here while I fetch a cab. You will catch cold outside.'

But she would not listen to him and hurried down the staircase. They went out into the street, but there was no cab to be seen. They continued their search, vainly hailing drivers whom they caught sight of in the distance. Shivering with cold and in desperation they made their way towards the Seine. At last, on the quay, they found one of those old vehicles which are only seen in Paris after nightfall, as if ashamed to display their shabbiness by daylight.

The cab took them to their door in the Rue des Martyrs and they gloomily climbed the stairs to their dwelling. All was over for her. As for him, he was thinking that he would have to be in the office by ten o'clock.

She took off her wraps in front of the mirror, for the sake of one last glance at herself in all her glory. But suddenly she uttered a cry. The diamonds were no longer round her neck.

'What is the matter?' asked her husband, who was already half undressed.

She turned to him in horror. 'I . . . I've . . . lost Madam Forestier's necklace.'

He started in dismay. 'What? Lost the necklace? Impossible!'

They searched the pleats of the gown, the folds of the cloak, and all the pockets, but in vain.

'You are sure you had it on when you came away from the ball?'

'Yes, I remember feeling it in the lobby at the Education Office.'

'But if you had lost it in the street we should have heard it drop. It must be in the cab.'

'Yes. I expect it is. Did you take the number?'

'No. Did you?'

'No.'

They gazed at each other, utterly appalled. In the end Loisel put on his clothes again.

'I will go over the ground that we covered on foot and see if I cannot find it.'

He left the house. Lacking the strength to go to bed, unable to think, she collapsed into a chair and remained there in her evening gown, without a fire.

About seven o'clock her husband returned. He had not found the diamonds.

He applied to the police, advertised a reward in the newspapers, made inquiries of all the hackney cab offices; he visited every place that seemed to hold out a vestige of hope.

His wife waited all day long in the same distracted condition, overwhelmed by this appalling calamity.

Loisel returned home in the evening, pale and hollow-cheeked. His efforts had been in vain.

'You must write to your friend,' he said, 'and tell her that you have broken the catch of the necklace and that you are having it mended. That will give us time to think things over.'

She wrote a letter to his dictation.

.   .   .   .   .

After a week had elapsed, they gave up all hope. Loisel, who looked five years older, said:

'We must take steps to replace the diamonds.'

On the following day they took the empty case to the jeweller whose name was inside the lid. He consulted his books.

'The necklace was not bought here, madam; I can only have supplied the case.'

They went from jeweller to jeweller, in an endeavour to find a necklace exactly like the one they had lost, comparing their recollections. Both of them were ill with grief and despair.

At last in a shop in the Palais-Royal they found a diamond necklace, which seemed to them exactly like the other. Its price was forty thousand francs. The jeweller agreed to sell it to them for thirty-six. They begged him not to dispose of it for three days, and they stipulated for the right to sell it back for thirty-four thousand francs, if the original necklace was found before the end of February.

Loisel had eighteen thousand francs left to him by his father. The balance of the sum he proposed to borrow. He raised loans in all quarters, a thousand francs from one man, five hundred from another, five louis here, three louis there. He gave promissory notes, agreed to exorbitant terms, had dealings with usurers, and with all the money-lending hordes. He compromised his whole future, and had to risk his signature, hardly knowing if he would be able to honour it. Overwhelmed by the prospect of future suffering, the black misery which was about to come upon him, the physical privation and moral torments, he went to fetch the new necklace, and laid his thirty-six thousand francs down on the jewellers' counter.

When Madame Loisel brought back the necklace, Madam Forestier said reproachfully:

'You ought to have returned it sooner I might have wanted to wear it.'

To Madame Loisel's relief she did not open the case. Supposing she had noticed the exchange, what would she have thought? What would she have said? Perhaps she would have taken her for a thief.

. . . . .

Madame Loisel now became acquainted with the horrors of extreme poverty. She made up her mind to it, and played her part heroically. This appalling debt had to be paid, and pay it she would. The maid was dismissed; the flat was given up, and they moved to a garret. She undertook all the rough household work and the odious duties of the kitchen. She washed up after meals and ruined her pink finger-nails scrubbing greasy dishes and saucepans. She washed the linen, the shirts, and the dusters, and hung them out on the line to dry. Every morning she carried down the sweepings to the street, and brought up the water, pausing for breath at each landing.

Dressed like a working woman, she went with her basket on her arm to the greengrocer, the grocer, and the butcher, bargaining, wrangling, and fighting for every farthing.

Each month some of the promissory notes had to be redeemed, and others renewed, in order to gain time.

Her husband spent his evenings working at some tradesman's accounts, and at night he would often copy papers at five sous a page.

This existence went on for ten years.

At the end of that time they had paid off everything to the last penny, including the usurious rates and the accumulations of interest.

Madame Loisel now looked an old woman. She had become the typical poor man's wife, rough, coarse, hardbitten. Her hair was neglected, her skirts hung awry, and her hands were red. Her voice was no longer gentle, and she washed down the floors vigorously. But now and then, when her husband was at the office, she would sit by the window and her thoughts would wander back to that far-away evening, the evening of her beauty and her triumph.

What would have been the end of it if she had not lost the necklace? Who could say? Who could say? How strange, how variable are the chances of life! How small a thing can serve to save or ruin you!

One Sunday she went for a stroll in the Champs-Elysees, for the sake of relaxation after the week's work, and she caught sight of a lady with a child. She recognized Madame Forestier, who looked as young, as pretty, and as attractive as ever. Madame Loisel felt a thrill of emotion. Should she speak to her? Why not? Now that the debt was paid, why should she not tell her the whole story? She went up to her.

'Good morning, Jeanne.'

Her friend did not recognize her and was surprised at being addressed so familiarly by this homely person.

'I am afraid I do not know you—you must have made a mistake,' she said hesitatingly.

'No. I am Mathildle Loisel.'

Her friend uttered a cry.

'Oh, my poor, dear Mathilde, how you have changed!'

'Yes, I have been through a very hard time since I saw you last, no end of trouble, and all through you.'

'Through me? What do you mean?'

'You remember the diamond necklace you lent me to wear at the reception at the Education Office?'

'Yes. Well?'

'Well, I lost it.'

'I don't understand; you brought it back to me.'

'What I brought you back was another one, exactly like it. And for the last ten years we have been paying for it. You will understand that it was not an easy matter for people like us, who hadn't a penny. However, it's all over now. I can't tell you what a relief it is.'

Madame Forestier stopped dead.

'You mean to say that you bought a diamond necklace to replace mine?'

'Yes. And you never noticed it? They were certainly very much alike.'

She smiled with ingenuous pride and satisfaction.

Madame Forestier seized both her hands in great distress.

'Oh, my poor, dear Mathilde! Why, mine was only imitation. At the most it was worth five hundred francs!'

---

1. Examine the first paragraph of the story, how is Madame Loisel described?

2. How does Mme. Loisel feel about her station in life?

3. What four words would you choose to describe Mathilde? Which words would you use to describe M. Loisel?

4. Consider the details given us to describe M. and Mme. Loisel. How does the author show us the difference in these two people's attitudes? How are their values different?

5. Why was it so important to Mathilde to wear the beautiful necklace? What does she equate beauty with?

6. Was the party a success?

7. Why is it ironic* that the Loisels live on Rue de Martyrs? How is the ending of this story ironic?

8. Do you know anyone who tries to be something that he/she is not? What does this behavior tell you about the person?

9. Remember the couple in O. Henry's "The Gift of the Magi"? How are Della and Jim different from the Loisels?

Debate

As a class, debate whether you agree or disagree with the author when he states:

> "Women are dependent on neither caste nor ancestry. With them, beauty, grace, and charm take the place of birth and breeding. In their case, natural delicacy, instinctive refinement and adaptability constitute their claims to aristocracy and raise girls of the lower classes to an equality with the greatest of great ladies."

"The Necklace" was written in the late 1800's. While this attitude may have been prevalent then, is it common today? How can women today attain a position and status in life that puts them in control of their own destiny?

* Irony is the contrast between the expected outcome and the actual outcome.

Guy de Maupassant 1850–1893

Guy de Maupassant was born in Normandy, a region in northwestern France. Gustave Flaubert, the famous French novelist, was de Maupassant's god-father. From Flaubert, de Maupassant learned a lot about writing. He became one of the world's best short story writers. Writing in a simple and realistic style, de Maupassant often portrayed a pessimistic view of life. In ten years he wrote over 300 short stories, six novels and 200 essays and articles.

Journal entry:
> Sometimes an important part of a person's growth involves making a change. Have you ever been afraid to try something new or to make a change? Explain in a fully developed paragraph how that dilemma made you feel.

Tonia the Tree

by Sandy Stryker

Tonia the Tree had a wonderful life
In the forest of Higgledy-boo
In the night she spread breezes, in the day she spread shade,
And all through the year, Tonia grew.

Liggledy Birds made a home in her hair
Out of string, beeble grass and warm clay.
Wiggledy Worms crawled around Tonia's toes
And taught her the games that they play.

With work, fun, and friends, Tonia had a full life
And for years she continued to grow.
At first she grew fast, but as the years passed,
Tonia's growth lost its pace and grew slow.

Her leaves, once so green, took on a grey cast;
Her arms seemed to sag in all weather.
Instead of warm dirt, her toes struck hard rock
And soon her growth stopped altogether.

No one could say as a certainty when
This cessation of growth had occurred.
"Two years this Christmas," the Wiggle Worms said.
"Oh no, it was spring," said the birds.

Tonia's companions did little at first
But wear sad, worried looks on their face.
Some brought her fresh water and felt her warm trunk,
While others just felt out of place.

"Sick trees need special attention," one said.
"There's only so much we can do.
If Tonia has really stopped growing, I think
We should call the tree surgeon, don't you?"

Reluctantly, then, the others agreed.
A tree that won't grow must be sick.
They got on the Higgledy-Grapevine and said,
"Send the tree surgeon, please, and be quick."

The doctor arrived with a satchel of tools
And set out to see what was wrong.
She checked Tonia's tonsils and looked at her leaves
As she whistled a tree surgeon's song.

She listened and tinkered and looked at the tree
From all angles and every position.
Then she announced, "What she needs is a change.
It's as sure as if I'm a physician."

"The soil here just can't meet her needs any more.
And she's not learning anything new.
It's not that this tree doesn't love all you folks,
But there's not enough for her to do."

Continued

"I know just the place for our Tonia,
A space where she really can grow.
She'll become a tree we can be proud of,
A tree we'll be pleased that we know."

"Oh no," cried out Tonia, "don't move me.
I can grow **here** on this spot
If I just make my mind up to do it.
You go on. I'll stay here. Thanks a lot.

Maybe I just need a trimming,
Or a new coat of wax on my leaves.
I could hang some new nests from my branches,
Or tuck my arms into new sleeves."

The tree surgeon gazed at her patient.
"You're sick, but I know you're not dim.
You know growth doesn't come from the outside.
Growth only comes from within."

"But trees **can't** be moved," replied Tonia.
"I know that it's never been done!
We're too big. We're too old. We're too set in our ways.
We're just sticks in the mud, everyone!"

"You're much more than a stick," said the doctor.
"You have roots, you have leaves, you can grow.
You're alive, and that means you have options.
Trees can move. Trees can change. This I know."

The Liggledy Birds had been listening
And tried to ease Tonia's fear.
"We change all the time," they told Tonia.
"It's great fun to fly south every year."

"Oh, it's easy for you," Tonia told them.
"You have feet. You have wings. You can fly.
For *me* change means being uprooted!
It's a *gamble*, a *risk*. I could *die!*"

"We weren't born in mid-air," the birds answered.
"Once we were helpless like you.
Our moms and our dads had to feed us
In the nests where we sat dumb and new."

"It wasn't exactly exciting
To sit at the top of a tree
With a nest full of brothers and sisters,
Though it was safer than just being free.

But our parents were having none of it.
They *insisted* we learn how to fly.
They *taught* us, of course, how to do it.
When we *learned* it was 'Birdy, bye-bye.'"

"Are you saying that you, too, were frightened?"
The tree found this hard to believe.
The birds made it all look so easy.
Could she really have been that naive?

"No one finds change is that simple,"
The birds then proceeded to say.
"Feeling the fear is quite natural,
But you just have to change anyway."

"Okay," Tonia said. "Then I'll do it.
I'll take a deep breath and I'll go.
It's all right, Doc, you have my permission.
It's once again time that I grow."

Continued

The very next morning it happened.
The tree surgeon came before dawn
With her higa-mejiggle machinery
And a truck to put Tonia on.

"You'll soon feel much better," she promised
As she dug all around in the dirt.
"Be a brave tree. We'll all help you.
I promise it really won't hurt."

All the trees in the forest stood silent
As the truck carrying Tonia passed.
Would it work? Could she grow? Oh, they hoped so!
She must *resume* growing at last!

Before Tonia knew what had happened,
The truck slowly came to a stop.
"This is it, your new home," said the doctor.
"You'll live here, on the hill. Near the top."

"It's a beautiful site," she admitted.
"Maybe this won't be so bad."
Then she wriggled her toes in excitement
And the birds thought she grew...just a tad.

The sun had come out now to greet her,
And help Tonia know she belonged.
And at night there was rain touched with stardust
To help the weak tree become strong.

The air on the hill was a tonic.
Tonia had to admit it was so.
She loved how it made her arms jiggle
While her feet remained anchored below.

Soon Tonia felt something happen—
Something vaguely familiar, yet new.
"New leaves," cried the birds. "Hey, you're growing!"
Tonia laughed, then she looked. It was true!

As she dug her toes deep in the soil,
Tonia flung her long arms toward the sun.
Once more the tree seemed to be changing
And she cried, "Look at me! This is fun!"

"Well," said the birds who'd stayed with her,
"If you don't mind, we'll be moving along.
We're due to fly south," they told Tonia.
Tonia smiled and said, "thanks." They were gone.

Then in silent salute to her comrades
Who had taught her so much, Tonia turned
Her leaves red, fiery orange and bright yellow
To show just how much she had learned.

Other trees on the hill looked at Tonia.
"Oh, how pretty, how lovely," they said.
"Green is a nice enough color,
But how grand for a tree to be red!"

Soon all the trees began changing
And the hill turned a rainbow of leaves.
Leaves of red, leaves of orange, leaves of yellow—
What bright patterns a hillside can weave!

That, though, was just the beginning.
Next Tonia decided to shed
Her jacket of multiple colors
To be used on the ground as a bed

Continued

For the Wiggledy Worms who were weary,
For the bumbles and beetles to nest.
Then all through the winter she stood there
To take a well-earned woody rest.

In the spring when the sun became warmer
And new life poked its head from the ground,
Tonia's limbs began bursting with blossoms
That launched sweet perfume skyward bound.

The scent soon attracted attention
To the tree with such beauty to lend.
Other creatures came 'round just to see her,
And most of them stayed to be friends.

"How could anyone fail to love Tonia,"
A friend in the forest reflects.
"She's so brave and so smart and creative.
You never know what she'll do next!"

"Till she came around, life was boring.
We all did the same dead, dull things.
Tonia's change has been our inspiration.
What once was a worm now has wings!

Raindrops adopted new patterns.
Flowers have turned into fruit.
Even the tiniest seeds in the ground
Are shoving out confident shoots."

Now all through the forest where once little changed,
Change has become a tradition.
Growth is encouraged, new goals are pursued,
And dreams are all brought to fruition.

"Don't be frightened of change," Tonia says now.
"Change is what helps you to grow.
It makes for a life of adventure.
　Just ask me.
　　I'll tell you.
　　　I should know."

---

1. Why did Tonia stop growing?

2. What did the tree surgeon decide that Tonia needed? What kinds of excuses did Tonia use to try to avoid the change?

3. Re-examine the advice that the tree surgeon gave; why did she suggest a change? What advice did the birds give?

4. Why did Tonia fear making a move? What did change mean to Tonia? What might have happened to Tonia if she hadn't moved?

5. Where did Tonia get her support in order to have enough courage to make the move? Do you think it is helpful to have support from family and friends when you are about to make a change?

6. What major changes do you anticipate in the next three to five years? What advice would Tonia give you about change?

7. Review "The Employee of the Twenty-First Century" on pages 242 to 245 of *Career Choices*. Quiz questions 6 and 7 on page 243 relate to your feelings about change. Do you embrace change, or are you resistant to it?

8. Sometimes our reluctance to change can limit the opportunities available to us. Review your responses to #7 and write three objectives to help you manage the change you anticipate.

Allegory

An allegory is a literary, dramatic or pictorial representation with two levels of meaning, one is literal and the other is symbolic. On the surface the work may appear superficial but it illustrates a deeper message. The events and characters in the story are symbols for ideas, concepts and morals.

Tonia the Tree is an allegory. Why did the author choose a tree to convey the message of change? Can you think of other "symbols" of change that might be used to convey the same message?

Extra Credit

Have you ever wanted to write children's stories? Write a short allegory for a favorite child in your life. First choose the message or moral you want to convey and then brainstorm possible characters and storylines that illustrate this message. Consider working in editorial teams. Two, three or four minds working on this challenge may make this assignment more enjoyable. Be creative! Have fun!

Sandy Stryker 1949–

Sandy Stryker was born in Willmar, Minnesota. She attended the University of Minnesota, where she earned a bachelor's degree in journalism. She is the co-author of **Career Choices** and a number of other books on career and life planning, and has also worked as a journalist and an advertising copywriter. *Tonia the Tree*, published as a children's picture book, was her first attempt to use professionally a skill she had always considered just a hobby — writing light verse. The book received the Friends of American Writers merit award in 1988.

Journal entry:
> Think about a job in which you have worked with others as a team (paid, volunteer or school related). What kind of people do you like to work with the most? Make a list of the traits that would describe these people. Review pages 238-241 of *Career Choices* for a synopsis of positive and negative work values.

To Be of Use

by Marge Piercy

The people I love the best
jump into work head first
without dallying in the shallows
and swim off with sure strokes almost out of sight.
They seem to become natives of that element,
the black sleek heads of seals
bouncing like half-submerged balls.

I love people who harness themselves, an ox to a heavy cart,
who pull like water buffalo, with massive patience,
who strain in the mud and the muck to move things forward,
who do what has to be done, again and again.

I want to be with people who submerge
in the task, who go into the fields to harvest
and work in a row and pass the bags along.
who are not parlor generals and field deserters
but move in a common rhythm
when the food must come in or the fire be put out.

Continued

The work of the world is common as mud.
Botched, it smears the hands, crumbles to dust.
But the thing worth doing well done
has a shape that satisfies, clean and evident.
Greek amphoras for wine or oil.
Hopi vases that held corn, are put in museums
but you know they were made to be used.
The pitcher cries for water to carry
and a person for work that is real.

---

1. What kind of people does the author like best?
2. What literary techniques (simile, metaphor, hyperbole) were used to describe these people? Find the images (list the line number) and identify them by using these letters:

   s = simile

   m = metaphor

   h = hyperbole

   example:

   line 8   "the black sleek heads of seals"   m

3. It's obvious that Marge Piercy appreciates certain qualities in people; what does this tell us about her values?
4. Do you agree that, "The work of the world is common as mud"? Support your opinion by using specific examples and answering in complete sentences.
5. Why are the references to ancient cultures important?
6. What does this author believe is "real" work?

7. Every group of people has a work ethic that is unique to its particular values and world view. (Maybe you have heard of the "Puritan work ethic.") We learned our work ethic from our parents' attitudes toward work, and what they told us, as well as from other adults who were/are important influences in our lives. Ask one of your parents what work ethic he or she learned as a youth. What influence has this ethic had on his or her life? Report back to the class with a summary of your findings from the interview.

Marge Piercy 1945–

Marge Piercy is the author of ten books of poetry and nine novels. *Circles on the Water* contains selections from her books as well as some poems never before published. She lives with her husband in Wellfleet, Massachusetts.

Journal Entry:
> Read page 246 in *Career Choices*. As a class, debate the Booker T. Washington quotation: "There is as much dignity in tilling a field as in writing a poem." Is it true, or do we value certain jobs more than others in our culture?

Be the Best of Whatever You Are

by Douglas Malloch

If you can't be a pine on the top of the hill,
  Be a scrub in the valley—but be
the best little scrub by the side of the rill;
  Be a bush if you can't be a tree.

If you can't be a bush be a bit of the grass,
  And some highway happier make;
If you can't be a muskie then just be a bass—
  But the liveliest bass in the lake!

We can't all be captains, we've got to be crew,
  There's something for all of us here,
There's big work to do, and there's lesser to do,
  And the task you must do is the near.

If you can't be a highway then just be a trail,
  If you can't be the sun be a star;
It isn't by size that you win or you fail—
  Be the best of whatever you are!

1. Do you agree with the philosophy expressed in this poem?
2. Think about a job or task you've completed that required your very best work. How did you feel about yourself after you finished the job? Describe the feeling in writing.
3. Complete the following sentences:

   If you can't be a (X) be a _____

   (X)
   ship
   lion
   eagle
   mountain
   rock star
   doctor
   professor
   carpenter
   manager
   contractor
   politician
   principal
   waitperson
   police officer
   lieutenant

Journal entry:
> Many times we see small children setting up a lemonade stand or selling things door to door in their neighborhoods to try to earn some money. Try to remember what your ideas were about wealth when you were a child. What did you think about money? Was money important to you? Did you ever try to earn it yourself?

Looking for Work

by Gary Soto

One July, while killing ants on the kitchen sink with a rolled newspaper, I had a nine-year-old's vision of wealth that would save us from ourselves. For weeks I had drunk Kool-Aid and watched morning reruns of *Father Knows Best*, whose family was so uncomplicated in its routine that I very much wanted to imitate it. The first step was to get my brother and sister to wear shoes at dinner.

"Come on, Rick—come on, Deb," I whined. But Rick mimicked me and the same day that I asked him to wear shoes he came to the dinner table in only his swim trunks. My mother didn't notice, nor did my sister, as we sat to eat our beans and tortillas in the stifling heat of our kitchen. We all gleamed like cellophane, wiping the sweat from our brows with the backs of our hands as we talked about the day: Frankie our neighbor was beat up by Faustino; the swimming pool at the playground would be closed for a day because the pump was broken.

Such was our life. So that morning, while doing-in the train of ants which arrived each day, I decided to become wealthy, and right away! After downing a bowl of cereal, I took a rake from the garage and started up the block to look for work.

We lived on an ordinary block of mostly working class people: warehousemen, egg candlers, welders, mechanics, and a union plumber. And there were many retired people who kept their lawns green and the gutters uncluttered of the chewing gum wrappers we dropped as we rode by on our bikes. They bent down to gather our litter, muttering at our evilness.

At the corner house I rapped the screen door and a very large woman in a muu-muu answered. She sized me up and then asked what I could do.

"Rake leaves," I answered, smiling.

"It's summer, and there ain't no leaves," she countered. Her face was pinched with lines; fat jiggled under her chin. She pointed to the lawn, then the flower bed, and said: "You see any leaves there—or there?" I followed her pointing arm, stupidly. But she had a job for me and that was to get her a Coke at the liquor store. She gave me twenty cents, and after ditching my rake in a bush, off I ran. I returned with an unbagged Pepsi, for which she thanked me and gave me a nickel from her apron.

I skipped off her porch, fetched my rake, and crossed the street to the next block where Mrs. Moore, mother of Earl the retarded man, let me weed a flower bed. She handed me a trowel and for a good part of the morning my fingers dipped into the moist dirt, ripping up runners of Bermuda grass. Worms surfaced in my search for deep roots, and I cut them in halves, tossing them to Mrs. Moore's cat who pawed them playfully as they dried in the sun. I made out Earl whose face was pressed to the back window of the house, and although he was calling to me I couldn't understand what he was trying to say. Embarrassed, I worked without looking up, but I imagined his contorted mouth and the ring of keys attached to his belt—keys that jingled with each palsied step. He scared me and I worked quickly to finish the flower bed. When I did finish Mrs. Moore gave me a quarter and two peaches from her tree, which I washed there but ate in the alley behind my house.

I was sucking on the second one, a bit of juice staining the front of my T-shirt, when Little John, my best friend, came walking down the alley with a baseball bat over his shoulder, knocking over trash cans as he made his way toward me.

Little John and I went to St. John's Catholic School, where we sat among the "stupids." Miss Marino, our teacher, alternated the rows of good students with the bad, hoping that by sitting side-by-side with the bright students the stupids might become more intelligent, as though intelligence were contagious. But we didn't progress as she had hoped. She grew frustrated when one day, while dismissing class for recess, Little John couldn't get up because his arms were stuck in the slats of the chair's backrest. She scolded us with a shaking finger when we knocked over the globe, denting the already troubled Africa. She muttered curses when Leroy White, a real stupid but a great softball player with the gift to hit to all fields, openly chewed his host when he made his First Communion; his hands swung at his sides as he returned to the pew looking around with a big smile.

Little John asked what I was doing, and I told him that I was taking a break from work, as I sat comfortably among high weeds. He wanted to join me, but I reminded him that the last time he'd gone door-to-door asking for work his mother had whipped him. I was with him when his mother, a New Jersey Italian who could rise up in anger one moment and love the next, told me in a polite but matter-of-fact voice that I had to leave because she was going to beat her son. She gave me a homemade popsicle, ushered me to the door, and said that I could see Little John the next day. But it was sooner than that. I went around to his bedroom window to suck my popsicle and watch Little John dodge his mother's blows, a few hitting their mark but many whirring air.

It was midday when Little John and I converged in the alley, the sun blazing in the high nineties, and he suggested that we go to Roosevelt High School to swim. He needed five cents to make fifteen, the cost of admission, and I lent him a nickel. We ran home for my bike and when my sister found out that we were going swimming, she started to cry because she didn't have the fifteen cents but only an empty Coke bottle. I waved for her to come and three of us mounted the bike— Debra on the cross bar, Little John on the handle bars and holding the Coke bottle which we would cash for a nickel and make up the difference that would allow all of us to get in, and me pumping up the crooked streets, dodging cars and pot holes. We spent the day swimming under the afternoon sun, so that when we got home our mom asked us what was darker, the floor or us? She feigned a stern posture, her hands on her hips and her mouth puckered. We played along. Looking down, Debbie and I said in unison, "Us."

That evening at dinner we all sat down in our bathing suits to eat our beans, laughing and chewing loudly. Our mom was in a good mood, so I took a risk and asked her if sometime we could have turtle soup. A few days before I had watched a television program in which a Polynesian tribe killed a large turtle, gutted it, and then stewed it over an open fire. The turtle, basted in a sugary sauce, looked delicious as I ate an afternoon bowl of cereal, but my sister, who was watching the program with a glass of Kool-Aid between her knees, said, "Caca."

My mother looked at me in bewilderment. "Boy, are you a crazy Mexican. Where did you get the idea that people eat turtles?"

"On television," I said, explaining the program. Then I took it a step further. "Mom, do you think we could get dressed up for dinner one of these days? David King does."

"Ay, Dios," my mother laughed. She started collecting the dinner plates, but my brother wouldn't let go of his. He was still drawing a picture in the bean sauce. Giggling, he said it was me, but I didn't want to listen because I wanted an answer from Mom. This was the summer when I spent the mornings in front of the television that showed the comfortable lives of white kids. There were no beatings, no rifts in the family. They wore bright clothes; toys tumbled from their closets. They hopped into bed with kisses and woke to glasses of fresh orange juice, and to a father sitting before his morning coffee while the mother buttered his toast. They hurried through the day making friends and gobs of money, returning home to a warmly lit living room, and then dinner. *Leave It To Beaver* was the program I replayed in my mind:

"May I have the mashed potatoes?" asks Beaver with a smile.

"Sure, Beav," replies Wally as he taps the corners of his mouth with a starched napkin.

The father looks on in his suit. The mother, decked out in earrings and a pearl necklace, cuts into her steak and blushes. Their conversation is politely clipped.

"Swell," says Beaver, his cheeks puffed with food.

Our own talk at dinner was loud with belly laughs and marked by our pointing forks at one another. The subjects were commonplace.

"Gary, let's go to the ditch tomorrow," my brother suggests. He explains that he has made a life preserver out of four empty detergent bottles strung together with twine and that he will make me one if I can find more bottles. "No way are we going to drown."

"Yeah, then we could have a dirt clod fight," I reply, so happy to be alive.

Whereas the Beaver's family enjoyed dessert in dishes at the table, our mom sent us outside, and more often than not I went into the alley to peek over the neighbor's fences and spy out fruit, apricot or peaches.

I had asked my mom and again she laughed that I was a crazy *chavalo* as she stood in front of the sink, her arms rising and falling with suds, face glistening from the heat. She sent me outside where my brother and sister were sitting in the shade that the fence threw out like a blanket. They were talking about me when I plopped down next to them. They looked at one another and then Debbie, my eight-year-old sister, started in.

"What's this crap about getting dressed up?"

She had entered her profanity stage. A year later she would give up such words and slip into her Catholic uniform, and into squealing on my brother and me when we "cussed this" and "cussed that."

I tried to convince them that if we improved the way we looked we might get along better in life. White people would like us more. They might invite us to places, like their homes or front yards. They might not hate us so much.

My sister called me a "craphead," and got up to leave with a stalk of grass dangling from her mouth. "They'll never like us."

My brother's mood lightened as he talked about the ditch—the white water, the broken pieces of glass, and the rusted car fenders that awaited our knees. There would be toads, and rocks to smash them.

David King, the only person we knew who resembled the middle class, called from over the fence. David was Catholic, of Armenian and French descent, and his closet was filled with toys. A bear-shaped cookie jar, like the ones on television, sat on the kitchen counter. His mother was remarkably kind while she put up with the racket we made on the street. Evenings, she often watered the front yard and it must have upset her to see us—my brother and I and others—jump from trees laughing, the unkillable kids of the very poor, who got up unshaken, brushed off, and climbed into another one to try again.

David called again. Rick got up and slapped grass from his pants. When I asked if I could come along he said no. David said no. They were two years older so their affairs were different from mine. They greeted one another with foul names and took off down the alley to look for trouble.

I went inside the house, turned on the television, and was about to sit down with a glass of Kool-Aid when Mom shooed me outside.

"It's still light," she said. "Later you'll bug me to let you stay out longer. So go on."

I downed my Kool-Aid and went outside to the front yard. No one was around. The day had cooled and a breeze rustled the trees. Mr. Jackson, the plumber, was watering his lawn and when he saw me he turned away to wash off his front steps. There was more than an hour of light left, so I took advantage of it and decided to look for work. I felt suddenly alive as I skipped down the block in search of an overgrown flower bed and the dime that would end the day right.

---

1. Who seems to be the narrator of this story? (Look at the first Gary Soto story and biography that you read in this text if you don't remember it.)

2. What was his "nine-year-old's vision of wealth"?

3. How is Gary's family different from the family he so admires in "Father Knows Best"?

4. How does Gary go about trying to become "wealthy"? What opposition does he encounter to his plan?

5. The narrator describes his block full of ordinary working class people, what do they do for a living? What do the people in your neighborhood do for a living?

6. Why do you suppose that the author mentions the class at St. John's Catholic School?

7. How do Gary and Little John spend their time?

8. Why did television depictions of "comfortable lives of white kids" appeal to him? What did Debbie think about his attempts to be more like them?

9. How is David King's family described?

10. What is significant about the Soto family? Is money all that important?

11. What would "end the day right"?

12. At the end of the story, we see Gary's neighbor look at him, turn away, and then wash off his step. Why do you think Soto creates this image? How does it make you feel?

13. Gary Soto's work is highly autobiographical. This story deals with many issues involving money, cultural differences and status. What qualities did Gary exhibit as a child, that would lead us to believe that he would be successful in life?

Journal entry:
   Is there someone in your life who helped or mentored
   you? When you think about this person how do you
   feel?

The Bridge Builder
by Will Allen Dromgoole

An old man, going a lone highway,
Came at the evening, cold and gray,
To a chasm, vast and deep and wide,
Through which was flowing a sullen tide.
The old man crossed in the twilight dim—
That sullen stream had no fears for him;
But he turned, when he reached the other side,
And built a bridge to span the tide.

"Old man," said a fellow pilgrim near,
"You are wasting strength in building here.
Your journey will end with the ending day;
You never again must pass this way.
You have crossed the chasm, deep and wide,
Why build you the bridge at the eventide?"

The builder lifted his old gray head.
"Good friend, in the path I have come," he said,
"There followeth after me today
A youth whose feet must pass this way.
This chasm that has been naught to me
To that fair-haired youth may a pitfall be.
He, too, must cross in the twilight dim;
Good friend, I am building the bridge for him."

---

1. Can you think of a time when you mentored a younger brother or sister, or someone who was not as experienced as you. Why did you do it?

2. Do you see yourself in the role of the bridge builder someday?

3. List five adjectives that you would use to describe the bridge builder. Would you like to be known for these characteristics?

Journal Entry:
>Complete one of the following sentences:
>>When I was young, I once stole . . .
>>When I was young, I once thought
>>about stealing . . .
>>Once, when I was young, my friend stole . . .

>Now, use that sentence to start a journal entry.

Thank You, M'am

by Langston Hughes

She was a large woman with a large purse that had everything in it but hammer and nails. It had a long strap and she carried it slung across her shoulder. It was about eleven o'clock at night, and she was walking alone, when a boy ran up behind her and tried to snatch her purse. The strap broke with the single tug the boy gave it from behind. But the boy's weight, and the weight of the purse combined caused him to lose his balance so, instead of taking off full blast as he had hoped, the boy fell on his back on the sidewalk, and his legs flew up. The large woman simply turned around and kicked him right square in his blue-jeaned sitter. Then she reached down, picked the boy up by his shirt front, and shook him until his teeth rattled.

After that the woman said, "Pick up my pocketbook boy, and give it here."

She still held him. But she bent down enough to permit him to stoop and pick up her purse. Then she said. "Now ain't you ashamed of yourself."

Firmly gripped by his shirt front, the boy said "Yes'm."

The woman said, "What did you want to do it for?"

The boy said, "I didn't aim to."

She said, "You a lie!"

By that time two or three people passed, stopped, turned to look, and some stood watching.

"If I turn you loose, will you run?" asked the woman.

"Yes'm," said the boy.

"Then I won't turn you loose," said the woman. She did not release him.

"I'm very sorry, lady, I'm sorry," whispered the boy.

"Um-hum! And your face is dirty. I got a great mind to wash your face for you. Ain't you got nobody home to tell you to wash your face?"

"No'm," said the boy.

"Then it will get washed this evening," said the large woman starting up the street, dragging the frightened boy behind her.

He looked as if he were fourteen or fifteen, frail and willow-wild, in tennis shoes and blue jeans.

The woman said, "You ought to be my son. I would teach you right from wrong. Least I can do right now is to wash your face. Are you hungry?"

"No'm," said the being-dragged boy. "I just want you to turn me loose."

"Was I bothering *you* when I turned that corner?" asked the woman.

"No'm."

"But you put yourself in contact with *me*," said the woman. "If you think that that contact is not going to last awhile, you got another thought coming. When I get through with you, sir, you are going to remember Mrs. Luella Bates Washington Jones."

Sweat popped out on the boy's face and he began to struggle. Mrs. Jones stopped, jerked him around in front of her, put a half nelson about his neck, and continued to drag him up the street. When she got to her door, she dragged the boy inside, down a hall, and into a large kitchenette-furnished room at the rear of the house. She switched on the light and left the door open. The boy could hear other roomers laughing and talking in the large house. Some of their doors were open, too, so he knew he and the woman were not alone. The woman still had him by the neck in the middle of her room.

She said, "What is your name?"

"Roger," answered the boy.

"Then, Roger, you go to that sink and wash your face," said the woman, whereupon she turned him loose—at last. Roger looked at the door—looked at the woman—looked at the door—*and went to the sink.*

"Let the water run until it gets warm," she said. "Here's a clean towel."

"You gonna take me to jail?" asked the boy, bending over the sink.

"Not with that face, I would not take you nowhere," said the woman. "Here I am trying to get home to cook me a bite to eat and you snatch my pocketbook! Maybe you ain't been to your supper either, late as it be. Have you?"

"There's nobody home at my house." said the boy.

"Then we'll eat," said the woman. "I believe you're hungry—or been hungry—to try to snatch my pocketbook."

"I wanted a pair of blue suede shoes," said the boy.

"Well, you didn't have to snatch *my* pocketbook to get some suede shoes," said Mrs. Luella Bates Washington Jones. "You could of asked me."

"M'am?"

The water dripping from his face, the boy looked at her. There was a long pause. A very long pause. After he had dried his face and not knowing what else to do dried it again, the boy turned around, wondering what next. The door was open. He could make a dash for it down the hall. He could run, run, run, run, *run!*

The woman was sitting on the day bed. After awhile she

said, "I were young once and I wanted things I could not get."

There was another long pause. The boy's mouth opened. Then he frowned, but not knowing he frowned.

The woman said. "Um-hum! You thought I was going to say *but, didn't you? You thought I was going to say, but I didn't snatch people's pocketbooks.* Well, I wasn't going to say that." Pause. Silence. "I have done things, too, which I would not tell you, son—neither tell God, if He didn't already know. So you set down while I fix us something to eat. You might run that comb through your hair so you will look presentable."

In another corner of the room behind a screen was a gas plate and an icebox. Mrs. Jones got up and went behind the screen. The woman did not watch the boy to see if he was going to run now, nor did she watch her purse which she left behind her on the day bed. But the boy took care to sit on the far side of the room where he thought she could easily see him out of the corner of her eye, if she wanted to. He did not trust the woman *not* to trust him. And he did not want to be mistrusted now.

"Do you need somebody to go to the store," asked the boy, "Maybe to get some milk or something."

"Don't believe I do," said the woman, unless you just want sweet milk yourself. I was going to make cocoa out of this canned milk I got here."

"That will be fine." said the boy.

She heated some lima beans and ham she had in the icebox, made the cocoa, and set the table. The woman did not ask the boy anything about where he lived, or his folks, or anything else that would embarrass him. Instead, as they ate, she told him about her job in a hotel beauty shop that stayed open late, what the work was like, and how all kinds of women came in and out, blondes, redheads, and brunettes. Then she cut him a half of her ten-cent cake.

"Eat some more, son," she said.

When they were finished eating she got up and said, "Now, here, take this ten dollars and buy yourself some blue suede shoes. And next time, do not make the mistake of latching onto *my* pocketbook *nor nobody else's*—because shoes come by devilish like that will burn your feet. I got to get my rest now. But I wish you would behave yourself, son, from here on in."

She led him down the hall to the front door and opened it. "Goodnight! Behave yourself, boy!" she said, looking out into the street.

The boy wanted to say something else other than, "Thank you, m'am," to Mrs. Luella Bates Washington Jones, but he couldn't do so as he turned at the barren stoop and looked back at the large woman in the door. He barely managed to say, "Thank you," before she shut the door. And he never saw her again.

---

1. Do you think Mrs. Jones changed this young boy's life?

2. Mrs. Jones gave Roger $10.00 to buy his blue suede shoes. This was something tangible, in other words something concrete or material, something that could be seen and touched. What else did she give him? What intangible things? (Something that cannot be touched or seen. For example, happiness, joy, and grief are intangible things.) How did the author convey this?

3. Think about the person you identified as a mentor before reading "The Bridge Builder." Make a list of the things that person has given you—both the tangible and the intangible. Which were the most important things?

4. Complete a Character Analysis Worksheet for Mrs. Jones. Would you like to have a person like this for a friend?

5. Do you think Roger will ever steal again? What kind of life would you create for Roger if you could direct the next ten years of his life?

6. As a class, choose two students to play the roles of Roger and Mrs. Jones. Have them field questions in a way they feel the characters would respond. This requires that careful attention be given to the story. What information did Hughes give the reader about each of these characters?

Writing Assignment: Create a Dialogue

Delete the last sentence of Langston Hughes' story. Add the following bridge and complete the dialogue:

It was ten years before Roger saw Mrs. Jones again. One day while walking through the park he spied an old woman feeding the birds. His heart skipped a beat when he realized who she was.

"Mrs. Jones?" he asked as she backed cautiously away from him. "It's Roger, I tried to steal your purse long ago."

"Roger, is that you?" Mrs. Jones exclaimed. "Well I'll be! I never thought that I'd see you again . . ."

Journal entry:
> Try to remember some of the best advice or counseling you have ever received. Where did it come from? A parent? A mentor? A book? A poem? Write those words of wisdom in your journal.

If

by Rudyard Kipling

If you can keep your head when all about you
    Are losing theirs and blaming it on you;
If you can trust yourself when all men doubt you,
    But make allowance for their doubting too:
If you can wait and not be tired by waiting,
    Or being lied about, don't deal in lies,
Or being hated don't give way to hating,
    And yet don't look too good, nor talk too wise;

If you can dream—and not make dreams your master;
    If you can think—and not make thoughts your aim,
If you can meet with Triumph and Disaster
    And Treat those two imposters just the same:
If you can bear to hear the truth you've spoken
    Twisted by knaves to make a trap for fools,
Or watch the things you gave your life to, broken,
    And stoop and build 'em up with worn-out tools;

If you can make one heap of all your winnings
And risk it on one turn of pitch-and-toss,
And lose, and start again at your beginnings
And never breathe a word about your loss:
If you can force your heart and nerve and sinew
To serve your turn long after they are gone,
And so hold on when there is nothing in you
Except the Will which says to them, "Hold on!"

If you can talk with crowds and keep your virtue,
Or walk with Kings—nor lose the common touch,
If neither foes nor loving friends can hurt you,
If all men count with you, but none too much:
If you can fill the unforgiving minute
With sixty seconds' worth of distance run,
Yours is the Earth and everything that's in it,
And—which is more—you'll be a Man, my son!

---

1. What are your first thoughts or feelings after reading this poem? Quick! Write those impressions in your journal.

2. Which line or stanza has the most meaning for you? Use that verse to develop an essay or autobiographical incident.

3. As a class, spend a period reading the poem one line or phrase at a time and as a group sharing life experiences where that particular advice would have been helpful.

4. Imagine an individual who has all these characteristics, values or strengths. Would they be someone you would like to be friends with? Why or why not? What might their Character Analysis Worksheet look like?

5. Who might Rudyard Kipling have been writing to?

6. Imagine someday that you wanted to share this poem with your daughter, niece or a special young woman in your life. Perhaps you want to use it as a card or make a poster for her bedroom. Many parents today rewrite lines of nursery rhymes and poems to make them more inclusive. In your opinion which line(s) would need rewriting? Rewrite those lines.

Rhyming Dictionary

While some people seem to have a natural talent for writing verse, many of us struggle with it. Yet most people enjoy sharing their thoughts in rhyme or giving the gift of a personalized poem.

Go to the library or bookstore and get a copy of a rhyming dictionary. You will discover a useful tool that makes your task of writing verse easier. This reference book provides lists of words that rhyme with certain ending sounds. For instance there are over 300 words that rhyme with "run." The endings you would look up are *un, ion, on, one.*

There are also computer programs for would-be poets. Inquire at your school computer lab.

Rudyard Kipling 1865–1935

Rudyard Kipling was born in Bombay, India of English descent. One of the most popular English writers of his time with both adults and children, he wrote many stories about life in India, the Far East and Africa and about the British stationed there. Married to an American, he spent a few years in Brattleboro, Vermont. While there he wrote *The Jungle Book, Just So Stories* and *Kim.* In 1907 Kipling became the first English writer to win the Nobel Prize for literature.

Journal entry:
  Think about a star athlete that you know or have known.
  What is special about him/her? How is this person
  treated? Would you like to trade places with him/her?

Ex-Basketball Player

by John Updike

Pearl Avenue runs past the high-school lot,
Bends with the trolley tracks, and stops, cut off
Before it has a chance to go two blocks,
At Colonel McComsky Plaza. Berth's Garage
is on the corner facing west, and there,
Most days, you'll find Flick Webb, who helps Berth out.

Flick stands tall among the idiot pumps-
Five on a side, the old bubble-head style,
Their rubber elbows hanging loose and low.
One's nostrils are two S's, and his eyes
An E and O. And one is squat, without
A head at all—more of a football type.

Once Flick played for the high-school team, the Wizards.
He was good: in fact, the best. In '46
He bucketed three hundred ninety points,
A county record still. The ball loved Flick.
I saw him rack up thirty-eight or forty
In one home game. His hands were like wild birds.

Continued

He never learned a trade, he just sells gas,
Checks oil, and changes flats. Once in a while,
As a gag, he dribbles an inner tube,
But most of us remember anyway.
His hands are fine and nervous on the lug wrench.
It makes no difference to the lug wrench, though.

Off work, he hangs around Mae's luncheonette.
Grease-gray and kind of coiled, he plays pinball,
Smokes those thin cigars, nurses lemon phosphates.
Flick seldom says a word to Mae, just nods
Beyond her face toward bright applauding tiers
Of Necco Wafers, Nibs, and Juju Beads.

---

1. What is the theme of this poem? How common do you
   think this situation is? Do you know any people who still
   live in the glory of their past achievements?

2. Think about your friends and acquaintances. Do you know
   anyone who may end up like Flick Webb?

3. Complete a Character Analysis Worksheet for Flick Webb.

Writing Assignment

Imagine that you are a client at Berth's Garage and a
professional career counselor. One day while you are waiting
for Flick to change your tire, you have a discussion with him
about his future.

Write a dialogue between such an athlete and a person trying
to convince him or her that there is more to life than sports.
First free write, exploring what the athlete would believe. Jot
down ideas about approaches the other person might use to
counteract such beliefs. Then write the dialogue, making sure
it is consistent with the speaker's characters and attitudes.

Final Writing Project: Write the story of Flick Webb's next ten years.

The above dialogue got Flick thinking. He decided that he wanted more from his life and that he had the drive and the character to accomplish his goals. He decides to come to you for career counseling.

Based on what you know about Flick, what three careers could you suggest he consider?

It happens that one of your suggestions is a career Flick has been secretly and passionately thinking about. His eyes light up and you see more energy in his responses than you have since you saw him on the basketball court in '46.

What kind of training will he need? Review pages 267 to 273 of *Career Choices*. Write a sequential plan for training.

Review pages 274 to 277 of *Career Choices* and your analysis worksheet to help you with character and plot development.

Help Flick develop his ten year plan. (See pages 222 to 223 and 278 to 280 of *Career Choices*.)

Using the above action plans and character analysis write the story, either in the first person, as if Flick Webb were writing about himself, or in the third person, as Flick's career counselor, watching Flick proceed with his plan. Pay particular attention to plot development, sequence and character development. Try to write an emotional ending to your story, one that will move your readers.

John Updike 1932–

John Updike, novelist, short story writer and poet, was born and raised in Shillington, Pennsylvania. The son of poor school teachers, he managed to go to Harvard University and the Ruskin School of Drawing and Fine Art in Oxford, England. In 1955 he joined the staff of *The New Yorker* as "Talk of the Town" reporter and was a prolific contributor to the magazine. Many of his works deal with the small-town environment of his boyhood. Updike vividly captures the essence of life in contemporary America. He depicts ordinary situations and events in order to explore the more important issues of our time. His work offers significant insight into the significance of everyday life. *Rabbit Run* (1960), considered by many to be his best work, certainly his most famous, is a grotesque allegory of American life. *The Witches of Eastwick* (1984), was made into a motion picture. His collection of essays and criticism, *Hugging the Shore* (1983), was winner of the 1983 National Book Critics Circle Award for criticism.

Journal entry:
> Imagine your twenty-fifth high school reunion. What will your classmates be like? How old will you be? What will you look like? How will you have changed? What will you have accomplished?

25th High School Reunion

by Linda Pastan

We come to hear the endings
of all the stories
in our anthology
of false starts:
how the girl who seemed
as hard as nails
was hammered into shape;
how the athletes ran
out of races;
how under the skin
our skulls rise
to the surface
like rocks in the bed
of a drying stream.
Look! We have all
turned into
ourselves.

1. List the similes you find in this poem.
2. What is the author referring to when she writes "false starts"?
3. How have the people changed?
4. What does the following mean?

   "our skulls rise
   to the surface
   like rocks in the bed
   of a drying stream."

5. Speculate about what the following could mean:

   "Look! We have all
   turned into
   ourselves."

6. Will it take some members of your graduating class twenty-five years to discover themselves?

Final Class Project
Your 25th High School Reunion Booklet

Most class reunion committees ask you to complete a questionnaire or an autobiographical sketch of yourself before the reunion. The data is then collected and included in a booklet to be passed out the night of the event as a memento of the evening. Everyone attending can later read about what their former classmates are doing with their lives.

Imagine that it is twenty five years after your high school graduation. You have received your request for information about your life from the reunion committee. The request asks for either an essay or a poem which details the events in your life since high school. What do you hope to have accomplished in the next 25 years? Write an essay of no more than 500 words, or a poem no longer than 40 lines, assuming that your life has gone exactly the way you hoped and planned.

Publishing Your Booklet

As a class, form committees to create your class booklet.

Choose **two co-editors** who will chair the project. Their responsibilities include:

1. Developing the time-line.

2. Writing the goal and objectives.

3. Finalizing the job descriptions for each of the subcommittees below.

4. Call and chair meetings of the sub-committee chairs.

5. Chair the general class meetings as described in the job descriptions.

Sign up for the committee that interests you. Sub-Committees should include:

Editorial Committee—This group will:

1. Collect and review the entries from each class member.
2. Ask for edits and rewrites where necessary.
3. Decide on the order of the entries.
4. Write the introduction.
5. Submit final copy to the typesetting and design committee.
6. Solicit ideas for a title to be voted on by the class.

Typesetting and Design Committee—Its duties are to:

1. Work with the computer department of your school and typeset the document using desk top publishing techniques.
2. Decide on the interior design of the booklet.
3. Choose fonts (type styles).
4. Enter text into the computer.

Cover Design Committee—It will:

1. Organize competition for the design of the cover of the booklet. Make a selection of those entries submitted, or take a class vote.
2. Submit budget for costs to the Budget and Finance committee and make a presentation for approval. This will determine how elaborate or how simple your booklet will be.
3. Submit final artwork and boards to the Production Committee for printing.

Copy editing Committee—Duties are to:

1. Edit the final copy of the text submitted by the editorial committee before it is sent to the typesetting committee. This means checking for grammar, spelling, punctuation, etc.

2. Once all of the boards for the interior and the cover are done, complete a final copy edit of the boards to check for mistakes during the typesetting and design phase.

Book production committee—This group will:

1. Research the printing sources for the booklet. What is the most efficient and economical way to print? Does the school have a print shop? Will a large business in your area donate their services? Will you need to hire a commercial printer? What will it cost?

2. Work with the cover committee to decide whether you want to print the cover separately? Where and how?

3. Find out how the boards need to be completed to meet the needs of the printer chosen.

4. Present the final budget to the budget and finance committee for review and approval.

5. Work with the printers to complete the project. Oversee all work and approve final payment to printers.

Budget and Finance Committee—Duties are to:

1. Review all requests for budget approval from the Cover Committee and the Book Production Committee.

2. Make presentation to the entire class to have budget approved.

3. Complete all bookkeeping functions.

4. Collect payments from either students or fund raising committee.

5. Present final accounting to class. If there is money left over decide how to use it.

6. Figure the cost per booklet after all estimated expenses are collected.

Fund Raising Committee—It will:

1. Develop plans for raising money for the production of the booklet after the total budget has been approved by the class.

2. Make a presentation to the class for a vote.

3. Carry out the fund raising plans with the help of the entire class.

Distribution Committee—The group will:

1. Decide how many books need to be printed before the books go to press.

2. Decide whether to sell extra copies. Decide as a class who will you market to (parents, grandparents, etc.) and at what cost.

3. Decide who should receive review copies. Consider the Principal, the members of the School Board, the newspaper, teachers.
4. Write a cover letter and send/deliver all review copies.
5. Set up a distribution system once the books are printed. Keep records of total books printed and where they went.

Your Booklet and the Actual 25th Reunion

Be sure to save the original artwork from this booklet. Assign three or four individuals to be responsible for making this booklet available to your 25th high school reunion committee.

Possible ways to use it:

a. You might want to have a copy there for everyone to see. It will be a great conversation piece.

b. Have additional copies printed to pass out at the reunion.

c. You may want to summarize each person's vision and include a few of the lines with the actual story that they submit.

As a class, vote on how you want this material shared at your actual 25th reunion.

We Are a Success . . .

Robert Louis Stevenson

We are a success:

When we have lived well, laughed often and loved much. When we gain the respect of intelligent people, and the love of children. When we fill a niche and accomplish a task. When we leave the world better than we found it, whether by an improved idea, a perfect poem or a rescued soul. We are successful if we never lack appreciation of earth's beauty or fail to express it. If we look for the best in others, and give the best we have.

Index by author and title

About the Editors

Janet Goode

Janet Goode received her Bachelor of Arts degree in English and a teaching credential from the University of California at Santa Barbara. Her teaching experience has been in public schools in Southern California, where she has taught English classes at the secondary level, co-chaired the English department, helped revise curriculum and participated in staff development. Currently she is with Gateway Community School, an alternative education program for high risk students in Ventura County. She enjoys this challenge and is developing courses in Language Arts which help students improve their writing skills. She frequently makes presentations at conferences for teachers.

Mindy Bingham

Mindy Bingham received her Bachelor of Science degree from the California Polytechnic University in Pomona, California. She is the co-author of **Career Choices**, along with 14 other titles both fiction and nonfiction. Her books have sold over 750,000 copies and are printed in five languages. *My Way Sally*, a children's picture book she co-authored, won the Ben Franklin Award in 1989. As Executive Director of a large social service agency for youth in Santa Barbara, California for over 15 years, Mindy has developed and disseminated self esteem materials for thousands of young people.

The Editors wish to thank the following individuals for their part in helping to make this book a reality.

Seymour Silberstein of Santa Barbara, California, for his encouragement to undertake this project.

Jan Fritsen of Irvine, California, for the initial idea and the first pilot project.

Jean Mickey of Aspen, Colorado, for her research, ideas and energy that helped launch this project.

Our peer reviewers:

Bernie Burley, Educational Consultant, Grafton, North Dakota.

Eric Burley, student, Grafton, North Dakota.

James C. Comiskey, author and lecturer, San Francisco, California.

Rosemarie Deering, Ph.D., Curriculum Coordinator for Secondary Education, Kansas State University.

Kenneth B. Hoyt, Ph.D., University Distinguished Professor, Kansas State University.

Robert Shafer, Ph.D., Psychologist, Santa Barbara, California.

Sandy Stryker, Author, St. Paul, Minnesota.

Our book production team:

Shirley Cornelius, production editing; Pete Diamond, copy editing; Itoko Maeno, cover art; Christine Nolt, book design and typesetting; Dick Rutan and Jeanna Yager for permission to use an image of the VOYAGER on the cover.

Other books by Mindy Bingham and/or Sandy Stryker

Career Choices: A Guide for Teens and Young Adults: Who Am I? What Do I Want? How Do I Get It?, by Bingham and Stryker. Softcover, 288 pages. ISBN 1-878787-02-0. $19.95.

Career Choices and Changes: Discovering Who You Are, What You Want, and How to Get It, by Bingham and Stryker. Softcover, 288 pages. ISBN 1-878787-06-3. $18.95.

Instructor's and Counselor's Guide for Career Choices, by Bingham, Stryker, Friedman, and Light. Softcover, 208 pages. ISBN 1-878787-04-7. $18.95.

Possibilities: A Supplemental Anthology for Career Choices, edited by Goode, Bingham, and Mickey. Softcover, 288 pages. ISBN 1-878787-05-5. $9.95.

Choices: A Teen Woman's Journal for Self-awareness and Personal Planning, Bingham, Edmondson, and Stryker. Softcover, 240 pages. ISBN 0-911655-22-0. $16.95.

Challenges: A Young Man's Journal for Self-awareness and Personal Planning, by Bingham, Edmondson, and Stryker. Softcover, 240 pages. ISBN 0-911655- 24-7. $16.95.

More Choices: A Strategic Planning Guide for Mixing Career and Family, by Bingham and Stryker. Softcover, 240 pages. ISBN 0-911655-28-X. $16.95.

Changes: A Woman's Journal for Self-awareness and Personal Planning, by Bingham, Stryker, and Edmondson. Softcover, 240 pages. ISBN 0-911655-40-9. $16.95.

Instructor's Guide for Choices, Challenges, Changes and More Choices, by Edmondson, Bingham, Stryker, et al. Softcover, 272 pages. ISBN 0-911655-04-2. $14.95.

Mother Daughter Choices: A Handbook for the Coordinator, by Bingham, Quinn, and Sheehan. Softcover, 144 pages. ISBN 0-911655-44-1. $10.95.

Women Helping Girls With Choices: A Handbook For Community Service Organizations, by Bingham and Stryker. Softcover, 192 pages. ISBN 0-911655-00-X. $9.95.

Is There A Book Inside You? A Step-by-step Plan for Writing Your Book, by Poynter and Bingham. Softcover, 236 pages. ISBN 0-915516-68-3. $14.95.

All of the following children's full-color picture books are 9" x 12", hardcover with dustjacket and illustrations by nationally acclaimed artist Itoko Maeno.

Minou, by Bingham, 64 pages. ISBN 0-911655-36-0. $14.95.

Tonia the Tree, by Stryker, 32 pages. Winner of the 1989 Friends of American Writers Merit Award. ISBN 0-911655-27-1. $13.95.

My Way Sally, by Bingham, 48 pages. Winner of the 1989 Ben Franklin Award. ISBN 0-911655-27-1. $13.95.

Berta Benz and the Motorwagen, by Bingham, 48 pages. ISBN 0-911655-38-7. $14.95.

Mother Nature Nursery Rhymes, by Stryker and Bingham, 32 pages. ISBN 0-911655-01-8. $14.95.

You can find these books in better bookstores, or you may order them directly by sending a check for the amount listed plus $3.00 each for shipping to Academic Innovations, 3463 State St., Suite 219A, Santa Barbara, CA 93105. (805) 967-9915 FAX (805)967-4357. Allow 3 to 4 weeks for delivery. For more information send for a catalog.